The Perfect Florida Lawn

Published by Cool Springs Press, a Division of Thomas Nelson, Inc., P.O. Box 141000, Nashville, Tennessee, 37214.

Tom MacCubbin, 1944-
    The Perfect Florida Lawn: attaining and maintaining the lawn you want / Tom MacCubbin
        p. cm.
Includes bibliographical references (p.).
    ISBN 1-59186-064-4 (pbk.)
    1. Lawns--Florida. 2. Turf management--Florida. I. Title.
SB433.16.F6M33 2004
635.9'647'09759--dc22
                                    2003021651

First printing 2004
Printed in the United States of America
10 9 8 7 6 5 4 3 2 1

Managing Editor: Jenny Andrews
Horticulture Editor: Dr. Clint Waltz
Copyeditor: Sara J. Henry
Designer: Bill Kersey
Production Design: S.E. Anderson

Cover: top photograph by Lorenzo Gunn, bottom photograph by Thomas Eltzroth

Visit the Thomas Nelson website at www.ThomasNelson.com

The Perfect Florida Lawn

Attaining and Maintaining the Lawn You Want

Tom MacCubbin

COOL SPRINGS PRESS

Nashville, Tennessee
A Division of Thomas Nelson, Inc.
www.ThomasNelson.com

Dedication

This book is dedicated to Mom and Pop—my parents, Anna and Joynes MacCubbin, who taught me honesty, respect for others, and my love of the land, especially horticulture. It is also dedicated to my wife, Joan, who gave up a lot of together time so that you now have a great reference in your hands.

Acknowledgements

This book will help you have a long-sought-after, green but durable Florida lawn, thanks to the assistance of many.

Thanks to the University of Florida Extension specialists and fellow agents who have over the thirty-plus years of my career provided many bulletins, in-service training sessions, and information from personal experiences to keep me abreast of the culture and constant changes in lawn management. I am also appreciative of all their personal correspondence answering questions, testing soil, and diagnosing turf samples. Thanks also to the researchers of Florida and neighboring states who have spent years diligently testing and improving turf, studying the pests and associated controls, and writing the references used by county agents today.

I am especially appreciative for the opportunity to write the Florida edition of this book. The concept, basic format, and portions of the information you are about to enjoy were developed by Steve Dobbs, a former fellow University of Florida Extension agent. Way to go, Steve.

Thanks to everyone at Cool Springs Press and Thomas Nelson. Thanks especially to Hank McBride, who has faith in my work and encouraged me to write this edition. Also I extend much appreciation to Jenny Andrews who coordinated the writing of this book and then carefully read and edited the many pages. Thanks also to my wife, Joan, for the encouragement and advice that kept the chapters coming. I am also appreciative for the photos she added.

Lastly, thanks to all the residents of Florida and especially Orange County, who for more than thirty years have allowed me to be their Extension agent, a role that prepared me to write this extensive turf publication.

Contents

Foreword

Not many people remember when farm animals did the mowing. I am not that old but do remember staking a cow or goat out on the lawn to cut the grass and fertilize. It really wasn't a good mowing job and the lawn feedings were inconsistent, but it worked for busy farmers and it fed the animals, too.

Most of us today want a manicured lawn and a foot tickler to walk on. In Florida this is a challenge as our major grasses have coarse textures. They can be left with a more ragged cut after mowing and are not always soft when you take off your shoes. But this may be changing. New grasses are entering the scene.

Actually these are not really new grasses, but just new to you and me. Seashore paspalum has been growing on the coastal shores for more than a hundred years. And there are new bermudas and zoysias. There are new varieties of St. Augustine with shade tolerance, those that don't grow as tall, and some with increased pest resistance. Other turf types such as carpetgrass, centipede, and bahia haven't changed much, but can be very reliable.

You have to know what you are doing to have a good Florida lawn. For the most part, we have a warm climate with periods of plentiful rainfall, when the grass grows a lot, and so do the pests. You need to know how to manage the turf and what to look for in pests. A lawn without fertilizer is yellow and makes minimal growth. One with too much water and fertilizer grows too lush and keeps you mowing, and provides irresistible food for insects. If you have a good St. Augustine lawn, you have to stay alert for chinch bugs that can destroy a lawn in weeks. But so can other pests, and how about the weeds? And Florida has dry times too.

For this book, I have drawn from my experiences and those of many others to develop the best care program possible. Do I have a great lawn? Not always, but neither will you. Most of the time you will have a bright green pest-resistant lawn, but problems will occur. This book gets you off to a great start in selecting the right grass, and then guiding you through the care and pest controls needed.

Now more than ever is a critical time in the history of Florida turf management. Water shortages may mean not watering as much and accepting a less-than-lush-green lawn at certain times, but that will result in healthier grass in the long run. Learn to put your lawn on a lean program to conserve water, fertilize following modern guidelines, and spray only as needed to protect the environment. This book will guide you through these tough decisions.

I love my lawn but I don't want to be a slave to the grass. You are entitled to an enjoyable lawn with less work, too. Let me help. And happy mowing!

—Tom MacCubbin

Regional Differences

Florida is a long state, almost 900 miles from the tip of the panhandle to the last island of the Keys, and as you would expect there are climatic differences. Most warm-season grasses grow well throughout the state, but St. Augustinegrass is king. One big factor that affects the quality of grass is the winter temperatures.

Most turfgrasses grow year-round south of Lake Okeechobee to Miami, Naples, and into the Keys. Bahiagrass slows growth when the days shorten in winter, but keeps its color. The four remaining major species for this area, bermudagrass, centipedegrass, carpetgrass, and zoysiagrass, all need frequent mowing and remain a good green color all year.

Homeowners above Ocala and northward to Jacksonville, Live Oak, Tallahassee, and beyond can expect a brown winter look most years. Here the grass is almost sure to go as dormant as possible by December. Gardeners who cannot stand the straw-like appearance turn to overseeding with an annual cool-season grass to renew the green turf look.

Central Florida is in between. Bahiagrass lawns begin to slow growth and need fewer mowings by the end of October, but if the weather remains warm, the rest of the grasses keep growing. Many years lawns remain bright green throughout the winter, with only those in the colder pockets turned brown by frosts and light freezes. If the weather warms, as it often does, growth resumes and the turf can re-green during the winter months.

Northern sections of Florida receive the first frosts as early as late November and are not free of cold weather until mid- to late March. First frosts arrive around mid-December in Central Florida and are just about over by the end of February. South Florida hardly ever sees temperatures below 40 degrees, and the grass just keeps growing.

Gardeners in coastal areas have to deal with saltwater sprays and underground intrusion into their irrigation wells. Some inland residents also deal with pockets of salty water deep underground that rises to affect irrigation water during the drier months. In these areas it's important to select a turf type that tolerates the higher salt levels.

Home lawn size remains fairly constant at about 5,000 square feet, but concerns for water shortages in recent years may affect future plantings. People are being encouraged to plant only what they need for family activities and devote the rest of the landscape to drought-tolerant ornamentals.

Gardeners throughout the state are also concerned about turf pests and environmentally friendly ways to maintain control. Many pesticides have been eliminated and there is concern about the best management practices. New fertilizers are designed to slowly release nutrients and help prevent pollution of the Florida lakes, rivers, and underground aquifer that supplies drinking water. Good management of all turf is critical to keeping an attractive lawn and protecting the environment.

Soils

Florida soils are mainly sands—the official state soil is actually the Myakka fine sand. Most Florida soil looks like beach sand that easily falls from between the fingers. But there are areas of clay, rock, and organic soils too.

Only in a few areas of Florida are the clays extra heavy, resembling the thick sticky red to brown soils of more northern states. Gardeners with clay in their soils usually get the benefit of extra water- and nutrient-holding ability. They are often called red soils but most still contain considerable sand.

Rock soils made of nearly pure rock are found in a few locations, especially south of Miami and in the Homestead area. The rocks have to be crushed or good soil added to grow much of anything, including a lawn. These are alkaline soils and usually applications of minor nutrients are important for good plant growth.

Organic soils, often called muck soils, are usually found in the lowlands and especially near lakes. They are formed from centuries of deposits from previously growing plants. Many are poorly drained and often acidic. If you live in one of these areas, you will probably just have to live with the acidity level and adjust the use of minor nutrients to ensure good turf growth.

Still, most homeowners are growing their turf in sands. It's a porous medium that offers limited supplies of nutrients and little water-holding capacity. The average foot-deep layer of sandy soil holds about one inch of water. This is enough to supply the turf with about three days of water during the hot dry times and well over a week during the cooler weather. Of course, the deeper the root system, the longer the grass can exist.

Sandy soils in some areas of the state have an underlying compacted layer of sand, clay, or organic matter combinations often called hardpan. It may be a few inches to several feet deep. Hardpan creates a seemingly impermeable barrier to water movement and root penetration. In these areas drainage can be a problem during the rainy season, and gardeners may have to be concerned with standing water and turf decline.

Where the sands are extra fine they seem to repel water, often making watering the lawn difficult. Some blame organic acids that adhere to the soil particles and others say the bits of organic matter mixed with the sands cause the problem, but in any case water is rapidly shed from the soil surface. Here wetting agents may be needed to break surface tension and allow moisture to penetrate down to the grass roots. Aeration of these soils and then immediate watering may also help.

In the interest of the environment and conserving nutrients, all gardeners should have their soil pH tested and the levels of major nutrients checked (except nitrogen, which is highly variable). Many Florida soils have adequate to very high levels of phosphorus. To help maintain supplies of this nutrient and prevent algae growth in local lakes, phosphorus may be at minimum levels or absent in modern Florida fertilizers.

Hardiness

A good trivia question for gardeners is "How many hardiness zones are found in Florida?" Most will guess three and forget about a small portion of one zone in the Florida Keys. Zone 8 runs from the Georgia state line south through most of the upper third of the state. It can be cold during the winter with temperatures dropping into the teens, but hot during the summer. Sometimes the turf selection does make a difference in these North Florida locations. During very cold winters, residents have observed that 'Floratam' St. Augustinegrass, which usually does well throughout the state, is more likely to decline. Here centipedegrass is a favorite grass for many gardeners, but it may be slow to recover after cold winters.

Zone 9 encompasses all of Central Florida south to about Lake Okeechobee. Temperatures are much warmer, but during the more severe winters the grasses can turn brown. There are of course warm pockets where the grass is always a good green color. This portion of the state is very susceptible to surprise freezes, with mild winter weather suddenly interrupted by arctic cold. The turf is often caught in a stage of active growth and may be damaged. In this zone a grass may have more limited use because of pest problems such as nematodes, which restricts the use of centipedegrass, zoysiagrass, and bermudagrass in many home lawns.

Southward are Zones 10 and 11. These are the warmer areas of the state that may get a chill but seldom a freeze. Climate is not a limiting factor here and grasses are more likely to be selected for their ability to endure pests, difficult soil conditions, and drought.

Precipitation

Grass needs water and water is fast becoming a scarce commodity in Florida. It's not that we don't have lots of water, as the state is surrounded by the gulf and the ocean, but this is salty water—too salty to drink or use for most turf types.

Rainfalls are usually plentiful. Most areas of Florida receive more than fifty inches of rainfall a year. The problem is it's not distributed uniformly. Most rains arrive during the summer, the rainy season. From June through early September gardeners can count on a storm during the afternoon or evening hours every day somewhere in the state. But there are very dry times when the shallow lakes turn to dust and communities become very concerned about their water supplies, and rightfully so. Consequently, gardeners are being asked to conserve water, and turf is unjustly considered a water hog.

Because of limited water supplies, gardeners are expected to tolerate less-than-perfect lawns. They may have to water less and accept a turf that goes brown during the extremely dry and often hot March through May months. Gardeners are being asked to develop cultural programs that encourage deep grass roots with more drought resistance and to water only as needed, not on a regular schedule. Part of the trick to keeping a healthy, good-looking lawn is getting it through the dry times of the year. Following a good cultural program can help keep just about any grass alive and even green during dry periods.

Maintenance

A good maintenance program is the secret to the health and survival of your lawn. But it's probably not exactly what you think. A lot of good maintenance is done by just walking the lawn and remaining alert for problems. This is called monitoring. It's the modern way to have a good lawn without over-applying pesticides and fertilizer.

All grasses do not need the same care, so it pays to select the turf type carefully. For example, bermudagrass and zoysiagrass lawns are high-maintenance turfs, and bahiagrass and centipedegrass might be considered the "poor man's turf." Some turf types need more mowing than others and many have a long list of pests that you must check for throughout the growing season. Each Florida grass has its own care program of fertilizers and pest control. You need to know when and how to use the products safely.

Also you need to know when and how to water. And don't forget to check the irrigation system: One malfunctioning head can result in a dead spot during the dry times. Of course you also have to mow. Some grasses like to be cut short and others are healthier if mowed high. There is a lot to learn but don't worry, it's all in the chapters ahead.

For More Information

One place to go is your local University of Florida Extension office. They have well-trained Extension agents plus Florida Master Gardeners to help answer your gardening questions. Most also have clinic times when they examine specimens, test soil, and help with turf problems. Give the office in your county a call to find out when to stop by. Also ask about classes, local Extension websites, and mass media programs where you can obtain more gardening information.

While visiting the Extension office ask to check the available bulletins on Florida turf types, pests, and home lawn care. All the University of Florida Extension bulletins are also available at http://edis.ifas.ufl.edu.

Garden centers are also a great source of turf care information. Many employ certified horticulture professionals trained through the Florida Nurserymen and Growers Association. Look for the certification patches on their uniforms and ask them your garden questions. Garden centers are also a great place to check labels and compare products. Sometimes you can find a less toxic or natural product to use on your lawn that is kinder to the environment. Some garden centers also offer classes that provide turf care information.

University of Florida
IFAS Extension
1038 McCarty Hall, PO Box 110210
Gainesville, FL 32611-0210
352-392-1761

Extension Information and County Offices
http://extension.ifas.ufl.edu

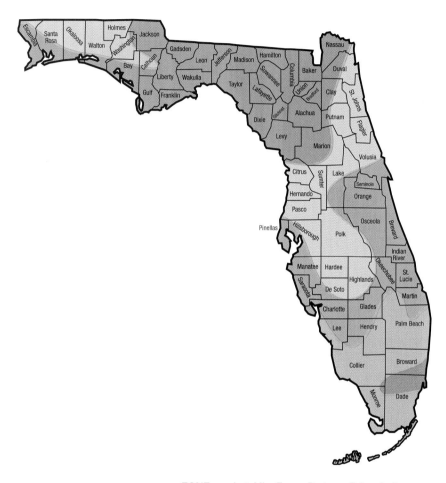

ZONE	Avg. Min. Temp. Degrees Fahrenheit
8a	15 to 10
8b	20 to 15
9a	25 to 20
9b	30 to 25
10a	35 to 30
10b	40 to 35
11	40 and Above

Total Annual Precipitation

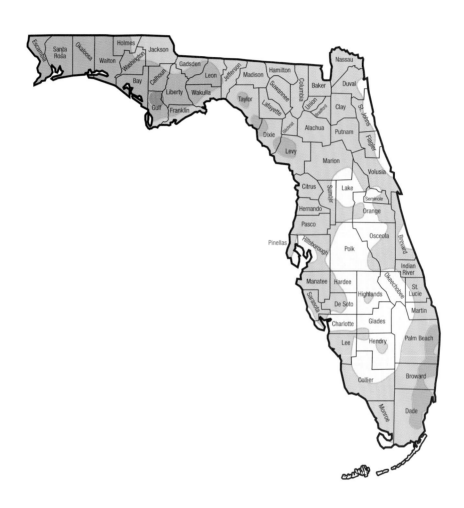

Inches

42   50   58   66   74

Oregon Climate Service, 1995

Florida Turf Maintenance at a Glance

Establishment

Seeding — March through early September for permanent turf; November through January for overseeding or establishing a temporary cool-season lawn.

Sodding and Plugging — Year-round when the weather is warm.

Renovating — March through November in northern locations; year-round in other areas when the weather is warm.

Dethatching — March through August in Central and South Florida; April through July in North Florida.

Mowing — Year-round, but mainly during the warmer months.

Watering — Year-round as needed following local restrictions.*

Aeration — March through October as needed.

Soil Test — Any time; complete analysis at least once. Soil acidity test every few years.

Insect and Disease Management

Scouting — Weekly during warm months; every other week during cooler weather.

Insects most prevalent — March through November.

Diseases most active — Look for different types year-round.

Weed Management

Preemergent herbicide for grass-type weeds — February as temperatures warm, with repeat applications as recommended on the product label.

Preemergent herbicide for broadleaf weeds — Late February to March, with repeat applications as recommended on the product label.

Post-emergent for broadleaf weeds — Year-round as needed following label recommendations.

Spot killing weeds with herbicides — Year-round as needed.

*Potable water is becoming a scarce commodity in Florida. Where possible use recycled water and stretch the time between waterings by irrigating only when the grass begins to wilt in spots throughout the lawn.

Planning and Starting a New Lawn

Chapter One

Survey the Site

Test the Soil

Observe Shading Patterns

Avoid Combining Different Grasses

Kill Existing Vegetation

Prepare the Planting Site

Choose Among Seed, Sprigs, Plugs, and Sod

Water New Plantings Regularly

Survey the Site

Landscapers tend to use turf freely when developing home sites. It's usually cheaper than adding lots of trees, shrubs, vines, and flowers, and it creates the bright green look we all like. But turf is not the perfect ground cover for all areas of the home landscape.

Some areas are just too dry, too small, too shady, and too difficult to manage for good turf. Really, the best idea is to use turf where it can make the most impact on the design and serve family needs for a play area. Whether you are landscaping a new home site or retrofitting an older one, you have to decide where you want turf.

A walk around the yard may help. Turf grows best in full sun. Yes, there are selections that tolerate some shade, but they all grow best with sunlight. Perhaps it is better to consider all shady areas "suspect" when considering how well you can grow grass. We will cover shade in more detail later.

As you survey the landscape, look for difficult-to-maintain spots, such as those two-foot-wide areas between the sidewalk and road. Small areas left between shrub plantings or flower beds and walkways are also problems. There must be something better than turf for these spots (turf alternatives are discussed further in Chapter Five).

Large open areas are best for turf as these sites are typically sunny, which promotes vigorous turf growth and offers good air movement to help reduce diseases. Also you can easily maneuver a mower in areas with smooth, flowing edges and as free as possible of trees, statues, birdbaths, and other obstacles.

Take a trowel with you when conducting a survey of your yard and dig down into the ground. What do you find? In most areas of Florida, you'll find just plain sand. But don't worry, this grows good grass. Our Florida varieties are accustomed to sinking their roots into these grainy soils. It also pays to get to know your neighborhood a little. Some soils have an underlying hardpan layer. This is usually compressed sand and organic matter forming a layer that is impermeable to water and

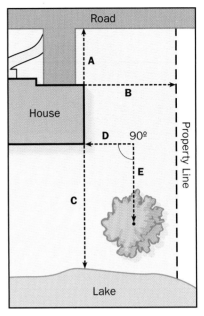

Calculating Lawn Area

roots. If you suspect a hardpan layer, dig a hole with a posthole digger to determine its depth and extent. You may have to live with the deep hardpan layers, but you might be able to disrupt any layers that are close to the soil surface.

When landscapes are poorly drained for some reason, you need to locate the low spots and try to drain the water to areas that allow better percolation, or to sites built to collect water, such as retention ponds. Most grasses need a well-drained soil to grow and look their best. Areas that collect water are likely to produce shallow-rooted turf that is susceptible to root rot and drought. It often turns a poor color during the rainy season because of the water-saturated soil. These spots, if not too extensive, may be best devoted to water-tolerant ornamentals.

Lastly, decide how much of a lawn you want to mow. Grass is fun until you become a March through November slave to the lawn mower. There are other ground covers that require less maintenance (for suggestions, see the list of ground covers in the appendix). They also may require less water and can help conserve this natural Florida resource. An attractive functional landscape usually consists of proportionate plantings of turf, trees, shrubs, vines, and flowers.

Test the Soil

Every lawn needs a soil test. Perhaps all you need is a simple acidity test to determine the pH, or you may want to test for some of the major and minor elements. A soil test will help guide your preparation of the ground before planting and future feedings throughout the year.

Collecting a good soil sample is the secret to obtaining a reliable soil test. Most landscapes aren't very big, and one or two samples may be all that are needed. Many gardeners sample both the front and back yards when testing. But if for some reason you suspect soils are different in other areas, take additional samples.

One soil sample should be composed of lots of smaller samples. It's best to gather the small samples in a bucket. Walk across the areas of the lawn to be tested and gather ten or more such samples. Use a trowel to dig down into the ground four to six inches and remove slices of the soil. Then mix these individual samples in the bucket. Take a pint of this mixed soil for testing. By mixing the smaller samples together you get a composite sample that is typical of the overall lawn. If you think one area of the lawn is significantly different, you can restrict your sample to just this section of the landscape.

Soil acidity tests can be obtained several ways. Reliable test kits are available from your local garden center. These do-it-yourself testers colori-

Take soil sample 4 to 6 inches deep.

metrically help you determine the soil pH. Readings below 7 are acidic and above 7 alkaline. Most grass likes to grow between 5.5 and 6.5, but pH levels up to 7.5 are often tolerated. Bahiagrass in particular needs a pH range of 5.5 to 6.5 to avoid iron deficiency symptoms.

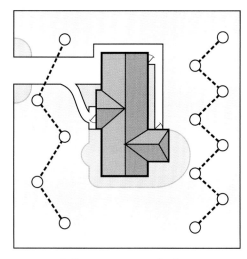

Collect separate samples from front and back lawn areas.

Many garden centers offer soil acidity tests either free or for a small fee. The tests are also available free or for a small fee from University of Florida Extension offices. Results of acidity tests are used to adjust the soil pH, which affects nutrient availability and the activity of soil microbes. Follow recommendations from test results to adjust the soil acidity with either lime or soil (agricultural) sulfur if needed. Retest your soil four to six months after treatment, or once a year if a treatment was not needed.

At least once, every landscape should have a complete analysis of the soil made through a testing lab. One convenient way to have this test done is through your County Extension office. Test kits are available for sending the sample to the University of Florida soil-testing laboratory. In return for a small fee, gardeners receive phosphorus, potassium, calcium, and magnesium data, plus the acidity test. Possibly the most important part of this data is the soil phosphorus level. If adequate, phosphorus may seldom be needed in the fertilizer. This has become very important around lakes where phosphorus can be a major pollutant in the water and increases algae growth.

Observe Shading Patterns

Take a walk around the yard and check for shade. Actually you should take the walk several times a day periodically throughout the year until you learn the seasonal shading patterns. Perhaps you have noticed the sun is overhead during the summer but dips far south in the horizon during the

Be aware of sunlight patterns in your yard. An area with dappled shade will limit the type of lawn you can grow there. Certain varieties of St. Augustinegrass are the most shade tolerant of the turfgrasses.

winter months. This affects the light levels needed to grow good turf and ornamental plants.

Some areas on the north side of the home may never receive full sun. Even areas between homes and other outbuildings may be almost totally shaded no matter what the exposure. Areas near trees are usually quite shady, but the light levels here, too, change throughout the year. You may have noticed that grass near deciduous trees tends to grow best during late fall through early spring, until the tree's leaves return. The good growth could be because of the higher light level in those seasons.

Turf near a home may grow better during the summer when the sun is overhead and shining directly on the grass leaves. In the winter the sun is often hidden by the home or nearby trees and the non-shade-tolerant turf types are more likely to decline.

Sun is very important to good grass growth. All grasses do well in full sun—it's the shady spots where they are likely to have problems. One good general rule: If an area of the landscape has more than 25 percent shade, it may be a tough spot for grass. In these spots you have to select your turf variety carefully to make sure it's the most shade tolerant. In Florida this is usually one of the shade-tolerant St. Augustinegrass varieties.

Often lots of shade also means lots of tree roots, which will compete with the grass. Trees are very shallow rooted and grow where the turf is trying to anchor down and absorb water and nutrients. Sod and tree roots have a difficult time growing in the same place. In many instances it's best to keep the turf toward the outer edge of the trees and use ornamental ground covers, concrete paving stones (pavers), or mulch in the shadier and heavily rooted areas.

Selecting the Grass

If you are purchasing a new house you may be able to select the grass—probably St. Augustinegrass or bahiagrass. More realistically, you will probably have St. Augustinegrass, which for years has been the standard Florida lawn. It may be a real shock to see this coarse turf growing in your yard if you are a northern bluegrass or fescue fan. But St. Augustinegrass produces a deep green, well-knit lawn with just a little care.

Bahiagrass has been the least expensive turf for home lawns, mainly because it can be cut from pastures and used as home turf rather cheaply. It's a coarse turf, too, and tends to create a more loose-textured lawn. It's quite drought tolerant and has few pests. But gardeners do have other selections to choose from, including bermudagrass, carpetgrass, centipedegrass, seashore paspalum, and zoysiagrass. All of these turf types will be discussed in detail in Chapter Six.

Selecting the right grass for your lifestyle will be important. Maybe you have many outdoor family activities, like badminton, croquet, football, or even hide and seek games. Family pets may also create pathways, disturb grass runners, or do a little digging. These can all be tough on the turf and you will want the most wear-resistant grass.

In recent years drought has been of concern as potable water becomes a valuable and, in some instances, scarce commodity. Most areas of Florida are under some permanent restriction, even if it's only the time of day when landscapes can be watered.

Some questions now must be considered that gardeners didn't have to deal with in years past. How often can you water the grass? Can you afford the water? Do you mind a brown lawn for part the year? Suddenly the drought tolerance of the lawn has become quite important. Luckily most lawns have some drought tolerance, but they will turn brown if you have to turn off the water. St. Augustinegrass is the most susceptible to drought, because its exposed runners can be affected by hot dry weather if you cannot irrigate.

Shade tolerance of the lawn also has to be an important consideration. Usually the St. Augustinegrasses are selected for lower light locations. But even among types of St. Augustinegrass there are some big differences. Florida gardeners learned many years ago that 'Floratam' St. Augustinegrass is a vigorous grower in full sun but offers little shade tolerance. Check the information in Chapter Six for a variety that suits your light levels.

Lastly, what does your eye tell you? Do you want the finely textured turf look? Perhaps you would like a foot tickler that allows you to take off your shoes and enjoy the carpet-like ground cover of grass. These lawns often come with more pest problems and the need for more care. You have to decide just how much time you want to spend with your lawn.

Controlling Existing Vegetation

The time to take control of weed problems is just before installing a new lawn. It's best to think of weeds as two separate groups: annuals and perennials. Mowing and tilling the site might be all the control you need to do for annual weeds, but will not control perennials. These persistent weeds usually have underground stem portions or thick roots that live from year to year. If only tilled into the soil, most will survive to grow up through your new turf. In fact, tilling may just propagate a larger crop of the perennial weeds. Sedges, weedy forms of bermudagrass, torpedograss, and Florida betony, for instance, are tough weeds to control once the turf is established. It's imperative to get these weeds under control before the new grass is installed.

Digging and pulling the weeds is always an option, but often leaves living roots, runners, and underground storage portions in the ground that can resprout and reestablish the unwanted greenery. With the really tough perennials, the best control is a nonselective herbicide that allows replanting shortly after use. Several brands are available at local garden centers.

When using nonselective products that are labeled for turf renovation, they must be applied to the green parts of the weeds. They are not effective if sprayed on the brown foliage that might be left from winter injury, or if applied to the soil. Wait until the weeds begin to make new growth and then apply the treatment. A repeat treatment may be needed in a few weeks to control new shoots that sprout from dormant weed roots and crowns.

Further preparation for planting new turf can begin when the weeds start to decline. It is optimistic to think even the best controls are going to eliminate all the weeds. Stay alert to new shoots that can be dug out or spot-killed as needed.

Prepare the Planting Site

Start by mowing, raking, and disposing of the declining weeds and other vegetation. It's probably best not to incorporate this debris into the ground because it becomes tangled in tillers and may be full of ready-to-grow seeds.

21

Tilling the soil six to eight inches deep is always the best way to prepare the planting site. And now is a good time to adjust the soil acidity level with soil sulfur or lime if needed, as determined by a soil test. This is also a time when you can work in organic matter or other types of amendments into Florida's sandy soil. These can help improve soil structure and increase the water-holding and nutrient-holding ability of the site.

Adding amendments works well with gardens where the soil is improved before each planting. When planting trees, shrubs, and turf, the one-time treatments are definitely of benefit, but short lived unless a permanent material is incorporated into the sands. Organic matter additions decompose over time and usually can be counted on to improve the soil for a period of one to five years, making the work somewhat questionable if you're looking for very long term effects. Inert materials such as colloidal phosphate and clays are permanent additions and can improve the soil for an indefinite period, but they are heavy materials and take some amount of labor to incorporate into the planting site.

Organic matter additions can include peat moss, compost, manure, and similar materials found at garden centers and landscape supply companies. Some gardeners also like to add organic topsoils, found naturally in areas of many counties, also available from landscape supply sources. Make sure a topsoil addition is as pest free as possible to avoid introducing new weed and pest problems. Look for evidence of weed portions in the soil, or even insects such as grubs and fire ants. Colloidal phosphate and clays are available through fertilizer companies and building or landscape supply dealers. All amendments are usually tilled into the top six to eight inches of soil at the rate of one to two cubic yards for each 1,000 square feet of prepared area.

Fertilizer may also be added to the planting site before establishing the new lawn. This is the time to use the results from your complete soil analysis. If a major phosphorus or potassium deficiency was noted, till these nutrients into the soil before planting. Otherwise fertilizer applications can be delayed until after the seeds and turf begin new growth.

Tilling to prepare a planting site is always best. Some gardeners make the mistake of simply mowing down the old grass and weeds then laying sod over the top of the debris. Some get lucky, and the grass grows roots and the lawn looks great for a while. But often the layer of debris is so thick that it inhibits good rooting, and the grass suffers drought and related root problems later in the season. You can add plugs through the untilled soil and establish a new lawn. But growth of the plugs may take longer, especially if the soils are compacted, which makes rooting and watering more difficult.

Stop and Plan Now for Irrigation

Don't miss an opportunity to install a proper irrigation system before planting the new lawn. Irrigation companies, irrigation supply dealers, and home improvement stores can help plan the system. Check local codes to see how much of the work you can do and how much must be done professionally.

With so much concern about water use in Florida, a properly designed irrigation system is important. It's best to design an irrigation system with separate watering zones. Turf is a frequent water user and may need added moisture once or twice a week. Nearby trees, shrubs, and flowers need their own separate sprinklers because they have different water needs and can often go weeks without additional moisture.

Seed, Sprig, Plug, or Sod

How are you going to produce green Florida turf? Depending on the lawn type, you may have a choice between seed, sprigs, plugs, or sod. The method you choose may depend on the amount of work involved and the cost. Some techniques for establishing turf also take more horticultural skills. Lawns can be established year-round in Florida, but some techniques are more adaptable to certain times of the year than others.

Sod: Obviously sod produces an instant lawn and it can be installed year-round. It is also one of the more expensive ways to establish turf. It you are buying a home in a new development, the lawn will most likely be sodded. Sometimes you do get to choose the grass type but often it's already been decided. If you talk to the builder early enough you may be able to have an influence on the variety chosen. If you are having the home custom built you can probably select the grass and may be able to do some of the work to help save costs. Gardeners renovating a landscape or patching problem spots can also pick their favorite turf. Installing sod is work but it's a good project for family and friends.

Florida sod is usually cut in rectangular pieces twenty-four inches long by sixteen inches wide, called "slabs," and stacked on a pallet. A standard pallet contains about four hundred square feet of sod, but a few growers still stack

Sod Placement

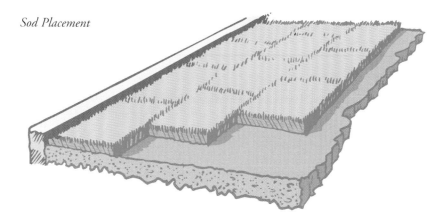

five hundred square feet to a pallet. Ask before you make the purchase and use the quantities to determine how many pallets you need. Measure the lawn site and if, for example, you need 2,000 square feet of turf, order five standard pallets. Most suppliers include one delivery charge, so order at one time all you need or can install conveniently.

Be ready to install the sod when it's delivered because it can decline quickly if left stacked, especially during hotter weather. As a general rule, it's best to install the sod within twenty-four hours after removal from the fields. If the sod is delivered and it must sit for a day or two, keep it in the shade and sprinkle the surface.

Installing sod is rather simple. Make sure the surface of the soil is raked or rolled smooth, and moistened an inch or two deep by running a sprinkler, then begin fitting the pieces together. Start laying the pieces along a straight edge and alternate sections so the seams are staggered (see illustration), to get a tightly knit lawn. Push the pieces firmly together to avoid gaps between the sections. Fill any spaces remaining with clean soil or sand. Water the new lawn as the sod is installed to keep it from drying out.

Plugs: Most gardeners choose plugs, which are approximately four-inch square or diameter sections of turf with roots and soil, for convenience. Trays usually contain eighteen of the approximately four-inch-square sections of turf, and can be stacked in a truck or the trunk of a car and easily carried to the site of a new lawn. When you do the calculations, the cost of plugs to produce a lawn is about two-thirds the cost of sod. Plugging can be done a section at a time and with less intensive labor than sodding. Lawns can be established with plugs year-round.

Plug Spacing	Number of Plugs/ 1,000 sq. ft.	Yards of Sod Required
6 inches	4,000	12+
8 inches	2,250	7
12 inches	1,000	3+

Some gardeners create their own plugs from sod with a sturdy knife. Figure that one square yard of sod can be used to cut just over three hundred two-inch-square plugs. Use the table on this page to help figure your landscape needs. Cutting your own plugs can help reduce the cost even more. You can develop variations on this technique by using strips of sod or pieces to fill in the barren lawn site, leaving some space between the sections of turf for new runner growth. Do fill in between the strips to create a level lawn, or bury the strips so that the soil line of the sod is even with the finished grade of the lawn.

Most plugs are spaced six to twelve inches apart to create the new lawn. They can be spaced further apart, but it takes longer for the lawn to fill in, and leaves the ground vulnerable for an even longer period of time to weeds that could invade the bare spots. When you get the plugs, you can borrow, rent, or buy a plug setter, which removes squares of soil the shape of the plug. Set the plug in the ground with the top even with the prepared soil. Some gardeners like to add a little slow-release fertilizer with the plug, but this is optional. Water after plugging and the turf is ready to grow.

Sprigs: Some grasses can be established from short pieces of runners, called sprigs, during periods of active growth, usually spring through fall. It's an older technique and the least expensive way to establish a lawn with

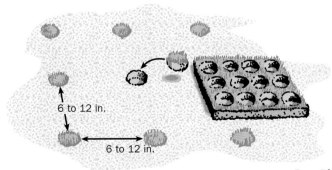

6 to 12 in.

6 to 12 in.

Grass Plug Placement

vegetative grass portions. The technique is somewhat labor intensive for home gardeners and seldom used to establish a lawn. But if you're on a tight budget, you might give it a try for small areas. This technique also helps maintain the original grade of the lawn.

Sprigging starts by separating pieces of grass into individual six- to twelve-inch portions. These are then set in furrows or pushed into the ground. One end of the sprig is set about two inches into the soil and the other end left at the top of the ground. The sprigs are set about six to eight inches apart. Another technique is scattering the sprigs across the surface of the soil and then disking them into the soil lightly or covering them with about a half inch of soil. After adding the sprigs, firm and thoroughly moisten the soil.

Seed: It sounds so simple, but seeding can be difficult for gardeners. Maybe it's because seeding has to be done when weedy species want to grow, too. Most seeding is done March through early September when conditions are best for the germination and growth of the grass. But you have to keep the soil moist, especially during the drier spring months. Seeding attempted during the dry times is a challenge, as the sites are often neglected and the grass shoots shrivel before they can become a lawn. Seeding is not for everyone, but it can be an inexpensive way to establish a lawn if you use your good horticultural skills.

Have the planting site tilled and moist but not wet. Decide how much seed you need and distribute it over the surface of the soil. To ensure the best

Seed Application Pattern

distribution use a spreader, walking back and forth across the prepared area to apply about half the seed, and then moving perpendicular to your previous path to apply the rest of the seed (see illustration). When applying small seeds such as those of bermudagrass and centipedegrass, it's best to mix it with some sand, soil, or similar product, so that it is easier to spread and is distributed evenly. After seeding, rake or disk the seeds lightly into the soil. Seeds can also be covered up to a half-inch deep with clean soil or sand. Many gardeners also like to cover the seeded area with a weed-free hay or straw mulch. Use about one bale to a 1,000 square foot area to lightly cover the ground. The covering can help retain moisture and control weeds.

Watering the seeded area is critical to the germination and establishment of the turf. If the planting site cannot be watered regularly, delay planting until the rainy season of June through August. A lack of water is the biggest reason for failure when attempting to establish a lawn from seed.

Post-Establishment Care

Every plant, including your turf, needs good care to become established. One of the most important needs is water. You could say "just keep the soil moist" but there's a bit more to it.

With sod and plugs it is probably best to follow the "rule of three." For the first week, water the turf every day. The second week, water every other day; and the third week, water every third day. By week four the turf should be well rooted into the soil and can be put on an as-needed watering schedule. At each watering, thoroughly wet the soil with half to three-fourths of an inch of water. And if the grass begins to wilt on those very hot windy days during the initial week or two, you may have to give it an extra watering.

Now, every rule has exceptions. Turf planted in more shady locations will need less water during the establishment period. Over-watering in such places can cause the grass to rapidly rot, especially during the rainy summer months. It's best to water just when the soil surface begins to dry. Also turf being established during the cooler months needs less water. You have to be the judge.

Lawns started from sprigs and seed have much different water needs. It's important to keep the soil surface moist while the seed and sprigs are rooting. Watering lightly but frequently during the first week or two is very important. When growth begins, start tapering off the waterings to every other day, and

Lawns not only provide recreational space and accent landscape beds, they also control erosion, reduce glare and noise, absorb air pollution, and trap dust particles.

by week three or four to every three days. Once the turf becomes well rooted, begin an as-needed watering program.

Help the grass continue growing by feeding shortly after the grass begins to root into the soil. Usually by the second or third week after sodding, plugging, or sprigging, the grass is running out of available nutrients. This is the time to do the first feeding using a general lawn fertilizer of a 16-4-8, 15-5-15, or similar ratio. Follow the label recommendations for lawn feedings. Lawns established by seeding can wait just a few more weeks. About a month after seeding, when the grass is up and growing, it's time to apply a similar fertilizer. Once the turf is established, resume a normal feeding program.

It's mowing time when the grass reaches the normal height for cutting. The ideal mowing time is when the grass grows about 30 percent above the desired height. If St. Augustinegrass or bahiagrass is normally mowed at four inches, then the mowing should begin when the new grass grows to just over five inches. Use a mower with a sharp blade and mow in a different direction at each cutting.

Newly plugged, sprigged, or seeded lawns are bound to have emerging weeds. It's best to try to mow-out the weeds. But some can be persistent. It's best to dig out perennials or spot-kill them with a nonselective herbicide, even if it means having to replace some of the turf. Do not attempt further weed control with herbicides until the new grass is well rooted in the soil and has experienced several mowings. Even then, read the product label carefully and follow the instructions for your lawn type.

Renovating an Older Lawn

It's rare that an old lawn is a total loss. Most likely some portion of the lawn has died due to a pest or cultural problem. Maybe chinch bugs damaged a section of St. Augustinegrass, or mole crickets damaged some bahiagrass. Perhaps part of the lawn did not receive adequate water and just dried up over time. Try to find out the reason for the decline and then decide if replacing the lawn is best, and determine the proper way to establish the grass.

Often in problem spots the area can be limited to a square or rectangular area that is easy to sod, plug, or seed. If the turf declined due to weeds, it's probably best to use sod. The sod covering the soil can help suppress weed seeds waiting to germinate.

Follow the same steps that you would take to start a new lawn by controlling unwanted vegetation, testing the soil, and tilling the ground. If plugs are to be used, it is possible to skip the tilling. But if the soil is compacted or consists of layers of old sod and organic matter, establishing a good root system may be difficult. Tilling the soil may also help disperse pest problems, and bury some weed seeds to keep them from germinating. Install the new grass and follow normal care to obtain good growth to quickly fill in the bare spots.

What Can Go Wrong When Planting a Lawn	
Over-Watering	Over-Fertilization
Under-Watering	Under-Fertilization
Cold Temperatures	Compacted Soil
Hot Temperatures	Seed Blew or Washed Away
Seed Planted Too Deep or Too Shallow	Damping-Off Disease
Poor Soil Contact	Site Too Steep, Poor Water Penetration
Improper Weed-and-Feed Applications	Dog Spots
Use of Preemergent Herbicide	Birds
	Insects

Watering

> *Know Your Soil Type*
>
> *Let Your Grass Tell You When to Water*
>
> *Water Deeply and Less Often*
>
> *Water Early*
>
> *Water Efficiently*
>
> *Condition Your Lawn for Drought*

Water-Holding Capacity of Soils

Did you ever consider how much water is available for turf growth in your soil? Probably not! The average sandy soil holds about an inch of water in the upper foot of ground. The water-holding capacity of soil increases with the addition of organic matter and clays. Some gardeners live in areas with lots of clay and some in areas with soils high in organic matter. These soils may hold more water for plant growth. They may also stay too wet during the rainy season or other periods of high moisture throughout the year.

Actually sandy soils are a blessing during the rainy season when there is a lot of water, and a curse during the dry times. It's always a good idea to determine what type of soil you have. For many gardeners this can be as simple as grabbing a handful of soil and allowing it to run through your fingers. If the soil trickles through as quickly as sand through an hourglass, it probably is sand. If it clumps up and does not break apart very quickly, it's likely a loam, clay, or organic soil.

Now dig down a foot or two into the ground. What do you find? If it's more sand, you probably have a well-drained site. If you hit a dark, hard layer, it is probably a hardpan of fine sand, organic matter, and maybe clay, which is often impenetrable for roots and water movement. This could be a poorly drained site during wet weather. Pour a bucket of water on this area. If it drains in a matter of minutes to an hour or two, you shouldn't have any problems. If it drains slowly over many hours, the area might become saturated during the rainy season and root rot problems could occur.

One other thing you need to do is sprinkle the surface of the soil with water. Many sands repel water when dry because of acids and organic matter mixed with the fine particles. If the water rolls off the soil surface, this could be a location that is difficult to water.

Simple Home Test to Determine Soil Makeup

For fun and to find out the real makeup of your soil, try this test at home. This is something you may want to get the kids involved in—it is just good basic soil science. As noted, Florida soils are mainly sands, but clay, silt, and organic matter could also be present.

Fill a jar that has a tight-fitting lid with a cup of the landscape soil. Then add water until the jar is two-thirds full. Now shake the jar for about a minute and let it sit. Observe what happens. Almost immediately the sand begins to settle out and forms a layer in the bottom of the jar. If your soil is mainly sand, this will be the thickest layer. When it appears that the sand has stopped dropping out of the solution, usually in a matter of minutes, make a mark on the jar at the top of that layer.

Now let the jar continue to sit undisturbed for a few hours and then note what has happened. You may find another layer of finer particles called silt. Make another mark on the jar. Now wait until the water becomes clear, which may take several more hours, even overnight. If another layer appears, it will be very fine particles called clay. (Sand, silt, and clay are the three major soil components.) Part of the soil mixture may be floating on the surface of the water. This is likely to be organic matter.

It's easy to determine what type of soil you have. First, decide approximately how much of each of the three major components—sand, silt, and

Home test to determine soil texture.

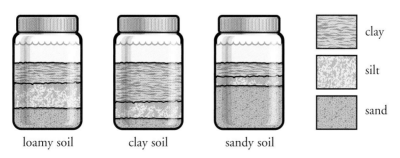

loamy soil   clay soil   sandy soil

clay

silt

sand

Soil Texture Triangle

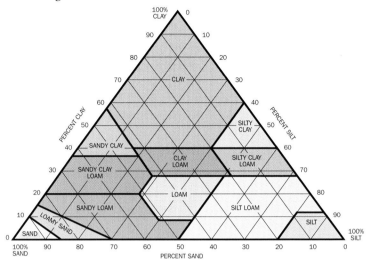

Source: Soil Science Society of America

clay—you have in your jar. Assign each layer a percentage. If your sample is almost all sand, then you have a sandy soil.

But suppose you have 70 percent sand, 20 percent silt, and 10 percent clay. What type of soil do you have? Use the soil pyramid to find out. Just follow the percent line on the side of the pyramid for each component until the percentages for each component intersect. Read the soil type from within the dark black lines. Note in our example that they intersect at sandy loam. This means you have a soil that has a little more water and nutrient-holding ability than just plain sand.

It's Time to Water

Everyone is concerned about conserving water. Wouldn't it be nice to have an easy way to tell exactly when it is time to water? You do, and it's the turf itself. Lawns have their own way to let you know when they are under water stress and need watering or rain.

Home lawns start to wilt when they begin to dry past the point that the roots can supply water. At first you might notice the lawn turning a gray green. Then, if you look closely, you will see that the grass blades are folded. This is a water-conserving response that keeps the blades from losing moisture. You might say the grass is wilting. If you walk on the turf or if you run a mower, cart, or spreader across the lawn, the tracks are clearly visible and the grass blades stay flattened. The grass is beginning to dry and the root system can no longer find the needed moisture.

You will probably also notice that the whole lawn does not become dry at the same time. Some areas exhibit the folded leaves and gray-green color before others. Maybe these spots have a shallow root system, or something buried in the soil could be preventing good root growth. Maybe the lawn has a nematode problem and the roots are much shorter in that area, or maybe other problems exist. Does it hurt a lawn to wilt just a little? Usually not. In fact, University of Florida studies show that a lawn that is wilting just a little grows a little longer root system. This means the roots can grow a bit further into the soil and possibly absorb some additional moisture. But you cannot let the turf wilt too much or for too long without some damage.

The best time to water is when you notice some spots in the lawn showing signs of wilting. Then water the entire lawn. During a hot, windy spring, this could be every few days. In the winter, the lawn could go a week or two without showing any signs of water stress.

Your soil texture, grass type, management style, rainfall, air and soil temperatures, wind, and humidity can all affect the amount and frequency of watering you will need to do.

How Much to Water

Determining how much to water seems to be one of the more difficult parts of lawn care. Gardeners often ask, "Do I water for a half hour, or how about an hour or two?" There is no way to just tell you how long to water. Each watering system is different and may put out different amounts of water.

Normally the recommendation is to apply a half to three-fourths of an inch of water at each watering. This should do a good job of wetting the upper foot of soil, which can hold about an inch of water. The turf cannot use all of this water, so this good soaking should be all that is needed, without wasting water.

But how do you know when you have applied this amount? Perhaps the best way is to place shallow containers with straight upright sides throughout the lawn to catch the water when irrigating. You could also use small rain gauges, available at garden supply stores. Whether you have an irrigation system designed for lawns or use a sprinkler and hose, this is a good way of determining if you are watering properly.

Catch the water in the containers for fifteen minutes and then measure the amounts. If you use rain gauges, you can read the amount directly. If you use shallow containers, measure the amount with a ruler. How much water did you measure in the containers?

Use the amount of water collected in fifteen minutes to determine how long you must water. For example: If you caught an average of one-fourth inch of water in fifteen minutes, you would have to water for thirty minutes to provide one-half inch of irrigation water and forty-five minutes to provide three-fourths of an inch of water.

Did all containers have roughly the same amount? If you noticed some containers had just a little water and others a lot, your irrigation system or sprinklers are likely not working properly or they are obstructed. Turn the system on and check for problems. A lack of adequate water—even when you think you are watering carefully—can lead to unexpected dry spots and declining turf.

Measuring Irrigation
Water Output

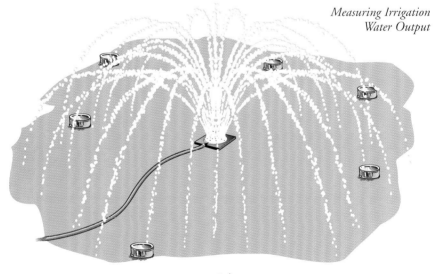

When to Water

Early morning is the best time to water your lawn.

Only in recent years has Florida had to deal with a lack of water. Water management districts and local communities have helped conserve water with regulations that restrict watering to certain times and days. Some are very restrictive because of depleted water reserves or limited resources. All are related to the amount of available water and season of the year. In most areas, watering is restricted and is not permitted between 10 a.m. and 4 p.m., which means no watering during the hotter portions of the day. Since the rules may be a bit different in your area, check with your water management district or your local University of Florida Extension office.

Actually it's best not to water during the hotter portion of the day, because then water can be easily lost to evaporation before it can infiltrate into the ground. Try to find a time of the day or night when there is little evaporation and little air movement. This is typically early in the morning. The best time to water is usually between 2 a.m. and 8 a.m. Gardeners with automatic systems can set the timer. Gardeners using hoses . . . well, you will have to get up a bit earlier or turn them on when you are getting ready for work. Timers for hose-end sprinklers can be purchased at home improvement stores and garden centers.

By watering early in the morning, you conserve water. Don't worry about wetting the soil during the night hours since it's almost always wet at this time from dew. Actually, by watering at night, you may even wash up to a tenth of an inch of dew water off the grass blades and into the soil, so the dew can help water the lawn.

Dealing with Dry Spots

Some spots in lawns are difficult to wet. Gardeners may say the water runs off the sand like water off a duck's back. What they mean is that the water does not readily soak into the ground. Consequently, the roots of the plants remain dry. Ironically, the best way to help wet these soils is to begin growing something like turf. The roots open up the soil and add organic matter as they

Select an automated irrigation system design that waters the lawn separately from garden areas.

decompose, which creates air spaces and improves drainage. But what do you do to help the turf first start growing in hydrophobic soils?

Improving the soil with organic matter and similar materials before planting can help, but it takes time and considerable effort. Most gardeners look for an easier technique, such as adding wetting agents to the water. Just sprinkling the soil with a few teaspoons of a solution of mild dish detergent mixed into a gallon or two of water can break surface tension among the sand particles and allow water to enter the ground. This can be done on soil to be planted or on existing turf. Do test your product a day or two prior to use as some detergents may cause burn. In such cases another, safer product might be selected.

Another trick is to use aeration techniques to punch holes in the ground to let in the water. It's best to use a core aerator that pulls a plug of soil out of the ground when run across the dry site. This helps loosen compacted soils that are slow to let the water into the ground. It also helps water to penetrate mats of roots often formed from dense-growing bahiagrass, bermudagrass, and zoysiagrass lawns. To be completely effective, however, you must water immediately after the aeration to get moisture into the ground.

Invest in an Irrigation System

Do you need an irrigation system to have a good lawn? Probably not. Many good lawns have been produced by moving hoses with sprinklers around the yard to wet the dry spots. A properly installed and adjusted irrigation system does help guarantee uniform wetting of the turf and good use of the water. It's also a convenience. Gardeners find it nice to be able to set the controller to come on at a specific time, often when they are still asleep. Or you might just turn on a zone as needed. Irrigation systems are very handy.

Many Florida counties now have extensive regulations concerning the installation of irrigation systems. This has become a job for the professional or at least the assistance of a professional. Ask for licenses and the proper permits before allowing work to be done on your yard. For the do-it-yourself gardeners, some companies will prepare irrigation designs and supply all the needed parts. This does not exempt you from local regulations and permits that might be needed, however.

If you are considering an irrigation system, have it installed before the sod or plugs are laid to avoid digging up good turf. Select a system design that waters the turf separately from the rest of the landscape. Setting up different irrigation zones for plants with different moisture needs is a significant way to conserve water.

Lastly, just because you have an irrigation system doesn't mean you have to use it all the time. Let the plantings tell you when the water is needed. Then water only the zones with plants that need the moisture. Monitor the water applied and check the irrigation system frequently to make sure it's operating efficiently.

How Much Drought Can a Lawn Take?

Perhaps another way to state this question is, "How much brown can you tolerate?" Most lawns are fairly drought tolerant, but if Florida residents are going to endure dry times, they may have to tolerate a less-than-perfect lawn. Keeping a lawn green and lush requires one to two inches of water per week, especially during hot dry weather.

When the sun is hot and dry winds are blowing, a lawn grass can use almost a fourth of an inch of water a day. Figure that a foot of soil, where most of the roots are living, can hold about an inch of water. This means the turf can use water available in the soil for about three or four days before it starts to decline. This also means the grass blades are going to shrivel and eventually turn a straw to dark brown color if you don't water. If you don't mind this look, many turfgrasses can survive the drought and won't need watering during normal dry times.

Many gardeners are facing this type of decision. With severe watering restrictions in effect in some locations, gardeners want the toughest turf for their lawn. They are also considering using grass only where it's needed for family activities.

It's ironic that the grass planted most often for home lawns—St. Augustinegrass—is one of the most susceptible to drought. Drought lasting for about a month can cause the turf to decline. Extended drought causes areas to brown and eventually die. St. Augustinegrass has stolons on the surface of the soil that dry rapidly, leading to decline. Centipedegrass and carpetgrass have similar growth habits and are affected similarly by drought. To survive much longer than a month, they need a water source.

DROUGHT TOLERANCE of Florida Turfgrasses*

Bahiagrass: *Browns but survives for months.*
Bermudagrass: *Browns but survives for months.*
Carpetgrass: *Browns and begins to die within a month.*
Centipedegrass: *Browns but survives for over a month.*
Seashore Paspalum: *Browns but survives for months.*
St. Augustinegrass: *Browns and begins to die within a month.*
Zoysiagrass: *Browns but survives for months.*

* *Without rainfall or irrigation during hot dry weather.*

Florida's most drought-tolerant turfgrasses are bahiagrass, bermudagrass, seashore paspalum, and zoysiagrass. All grow from rhizomes that are under the soil surface and are protected from drying. All can turn brown and survive months of drought, and regrow when the rains return or irrigation water is provided. Drought tolerance is one good reason for selecting a turfgrass, but you also need to research pest and maintenance needs to decide which grass is best for you.

Preparing Your Lawn for Drought

Florida is often dry from October through May, but the real period of severe water stress is during the spring. That is when grass begins new growth, the days grow hotter, and frequent winds dry the lawn. Luckily this only lasts a few months. The rest of the year is a good time for growing turf, often with adequate rainfall. Gardeners need a plan to get through the dry times—they need to drought-proof their lawns.

Like training a puppy to live in your household, a lawn can be trained to survive in your landscape. Water training is possibly the most important lesson for you and your new lawn. By carefully withholding water to encourage a deep root system, you can increase the lawn's drought tolerance. Every time the lawn shows just a little drought stress, the roots grow a little longer and extend a little deeper to reach the water in the soil.

Training can begin any time. One good time is just after the newly seeded, sodded, or plugged lawn has become established. Waste no time putting the lawn on an as-needed watering schedule. When you see spots starting to wilt a little, it's time to water. The best time to train your lawn is during the late winter or early spring when new growth is beginning. Get the turf accustomed to some stress, and water only as needed to develop a deep root system. When you do water thoroughly, wet the soil with a half to three-fourths of an inch of water to give the roots the moisture needed for good growth.

When mowing your lawn it's best to cut the turf at the uppermost limit of your mower. Grass cut at the recommended height develops deep roots (see Chapter Six for mowing height recommendations). This again ensures maximum water use. Also cut the lawn frequently and use a sharp mower blade. Chapter Four has further information on mowing.

When drought is eminent, reduce your feedings. If you cannot water, stop feedings completely. You can fertilize and promote growth later when water becomes available. Excessive nitrogen from fertilizer during the dry times can stress the grass and cause further decline.

Potassium has been associated with reducing stress and possibly increasing drought tolerance. New University of Florida recommendations call for increased potassium in fertilizers. Use of potassium levels (up to the level of the nitrogen in the fertilizer) is believed to help turf tolerate moisture stress. If you follow good fertilizing practices, you are probably adding adequate potassium during fall and spring feedings. If you think extra potassium might be needed, use a university soil test as a guide.

Some turf pests tend to be worst during drought. Chinch bugs are often more evident in grass that is not growing normally. Nematode problems are also more obvious as these soilborne microscopic worms damage root systems. Try to find pest problems early while the populations are small and easily controlled with spot treatments. Regrettably, nematodes are a severe problem and areas in the lawn may have to be replaced when good growing weather returns.

Ways to Save Water

Reduce Slopes or Berms in the Lawn

Avoid Runoff Situations

Test and Amend Soil

Add Organic Material as Topdressing Whenever Possible

Install a Water-Efficient Irrigation System

Select Drought-Tolerant Grass

Sod Rather Than Seed

Water Early in the Morning

Minimize Fertilizer

Mow High

Fertilizing

> **Apply Only What Is Needed**
>
> **Choose a Maintenance Level**
>
> **Apply at Appropriate Time of Year**
>
> **Don't Apply When Leaves Are Wet**
>
> **Don't Apply When Grass Is Stressed**
>
> **Split Rates in Half and Apply in Two Different Directions**
>
> **Water Summer Applications Thoroughly**
>
> **Be Careful with Weed-and-Feed Combinations**
>
> **Consider Organic or Slow-Release Products**
>
> **Do Not Apply to Driveways, Walkways, and Streets**

How Much Fertilizer Is Enough?

It's not a cure-all, but as just about every gardener knows, fertilizer can turn grass green. Fertilizer also, however, can promote excessive growth that leads to lots of mowing, aboveground runner growth, spongy lawns, and disease and insect problems.

Fertilizers are also being singled out as one of our major causes for water pollution in the state. Gardeners and professionals are being asked to decide if the feedings are really needed and how much fertilizer should be applied. Most Florida soils are very porous and nutrients can be washed through into the drinking water supply. Many nutrients can also be washed down streets into retention ponds and to the lakes.

So do you really need to fertilize a lawn? The answer is usually yes, but maybe not as frequently as you might think. Most lawns do quite well on a lean diet of no more than two or three feedings a year. Will you have a really green lawn with lots of growth? Probably not. But you will have a tough lawn—one that is more resistant to chinch bugs, diseases, and nematodes. You be the judge. If you were a bug, would you pick the green but tough lawn or the unusually lush green, easy-to-consume turf? Maybe that will help you find your answer. For most, the more durable turf is best for the home lawn.

New guidelines do establish various degrees of feeding based on nitrogen fertilizer applications—gardeners can pick from low, medium, and high maintenance levels. You have to decide what you want. Low to medium feedings are probably best for most home lawns. They are less work and may promote fewer pests. High feeding levels may give a lush green look, but the lawn could be the favorite feeding ground for insects, diseases, and nematodes—and expect lots of mowing. The turf may also need periodic renovation to keep the lawn from developing thatch and becoming spongy. Most gardeners don't need extra work and Florida definitely does not need fertilizers entering our water resources.

Soil Acidity and Growth

A soil acidity test to determine pH is the first step to good lawn care and proper feedings. Soil pH ranges from 0 to 14, and indicates the acidity of the ground. A pH of 7 is neutral and desirable for many plants. Soils with a pH below 7 are acidic. Most plants also grow well with a pH on the acid side, of 5.5 or higher. Bahiagrass and centipedegrass lawns especially like a pH around 5.5 to 6.0. At this level a significant amount of iron is available and the turf responds with a darker green color. All other turf types usually grow well in the 6.0 to 7.0 range. Soils with a pH above 7 are alkaline and lead to nutrient deficiencies with many plants.

Changing Soil pH

Raising the pH of Sandy Soils to 6.5

Existing Soil pH	Pounds of Dolomitic Lime per 1,000 Square Feet
6.0	0
5.5	20
5.0	30
4.5	40

Lime recommendations are minimal rates. Retest the soil after two to three months and reapply lime if needed.

Soil pH regulates soil microbe activity, root growth, and overall plant health. Its dominant role, however, is nutrient availability. As noted, iron is most available in the acid pH range. Acidity affects all nutrients. A pH of around 6.5 is considered ideal in areas where nutrients are most plentiful. At a soil pH that is too acid or too alkaline, nutrients become unavailable or toxic and plant growth can be affected.

A soil test is used to determine if the pH needs adjustment. If the soil is 5.5 or below, dolomitic lime is usually added to raise the pH. This form of lime also supplies needed calcium and magnesium. If the soil pH is properly adjusted, Florida gardeners normally do not have to worry about supplying these nutrients as part of their fertilization program.

Soils in the alkaline range can sometimes be adjusted by adding soil sulfur. If needed, it's best applied before installing a new lawn. Applying soil sulfur to an established lawn must be done in small quantities and is seldom recommended. Instead, gardeners can supply minor nutrients, often unavailable at the higher pH levels, through the fertilizer. Because of soil buffering capacities, which helps a soil resist pH change, making an alkaline soil acidic is also often impossible.

Many gardeners come to Florida from areas of the country where lime is used to adjust the soil pH yearly. This is not recommended in Florida. Have the soil acidity tested first, then decide if lime is needed.

Essential Nutrients

Plants need sixteen nutrients for growth. They obtain hydrogen, carbon, and oxygen through air and water. Most of the remaining nutrients are usually obtained by absorption through roots growing in the soil. Some nutrients can be absorbed through stems and leaves but foliar feedings are normally not used to supply fertilizer for turf growth. Most turf feedings are made with granular or liquid fertilizers that provide nutrients to the roots.

Turf also uses various macronutrients for growth, including nitrogen, phosphorus, potassium, calcium, magnesium, and sulfur. Of these, the first three are used in the largest quantities. Nitrogen, phosphorus, and potassium are the three parts of a fertilizer analysis noted on the fertilizer bag, such as 16-4-8 or 15-0-15. Nitrogen produces green leaf growth, phosphorus helps develop strong roots and stems, and potassium contributes to hardiness and overall vigor.

Recently phosphorus has been of major concern. Scientists have shown that excess phosphorus can end up in water supplies and contributes to algae growth. Phosphorus levels remain fairly constant in the soils and usually do not need regular adjustment. It's now suggested that phosphorus feedings not be made unless a soil test determines the need for this nutrient. Many home sites that have been fertilized previously when used for agriculture production or have had regular feedings for turf or ornamentals probably do not need additional phosphorus.

The two optimum times of the year to fertilize the lawn are spring and fall. Applications at other times may be appropriate depending on the type of grass.

The remaining nutrients needed for turf growth are called micronutrients, and include boron, chlorine, copper, iron, manganese, molybdenum, sulfur, and zinc. Many are plentiful in the soil or are included as a small portion of fertilizer applied to the turf. Some, like iron, may be applied as a special feeding. Micronutrients are just as important as the macronutrients, but are used in much smaller quantities.

What to Feed

Gardeners have lots of choices when it comes to fertilizers. Just look at all the bags of lawn food found at your local garden center. Probably any one of these products could feed your lawn and do it well. The question really becomes, "What does your lawn need for fertilizer?"

There is no doubt that nitrogen is needed to keep the lawn green. This is what makes the turf "green up" after the spring feeding. It also leaches out of the soil very quickly or escapes into the atmosphere. We will always have to add some nitrogen to have a green lawn. But are all the other nutrients as important? Do you need to supply all the nutrients, or are some already in the ground just waiting to be absorbed by the roots?

By now it's fairly obvious that a soil test is the best way to decide if you need two of the macronutrients, phosphorus and potassium. Many of our soils have adequate supplies of phosphorus and adding more is not necessary during regularly scheduled feedings. Will adding extra harm the turf? No, but it may affect the environment. Potassium levels can also be determined by the soil test. This nutrient leaches out of the soil and may not be available. You can use the results of a soil test as a guide, but most fertilizer recommendations now call for potassium levels ranging from half that of or equal to the nitrogen rate.

If the pH of the soil has been properly adjusted, the calcium and magnesium levels of soils are usually adequate. Here again a soil test will tell for sure. Most fertilizers usually supply micronutrients to guarantee that some will always be available. Iron is frequently added as a special feeding, to help with the spring green-up and summer turf maintenance.

Modern fertilizers may also have a certain amount of the nutrients in a slow-release form. This is a way to gradually supply the nitrogen and prevent it from leaching out of the soil. Look for products with the words "slow release," "controlled released," or "encapsulated" on the label to indicate they are that type of product. Other nutrients may also be in slow-release forms in some fertilizers.

Water your lawn after you have applied fertilizer, but not before. Applying fertilizer on wet grass can burn the foliage.

All lawn feedings are based on the amount of nitrogen applied to the turf at any one time. It's recommended that no more than one pound of nitrogen be applied to each 1,000 square feet of turf at any one application. Only one half pound of the nitrogen should be in a water-soluble form. The rest of the nitrogen should be in a slow-release form.

So what should a gardener buy? Unless you are a real fertilizer whiz, perhaps it is best to select a product high in nitrogen and potassium and low in phosphorus, such as those with ratios of 16-4-8, 15-5-15, 15-0-15, and 18-0-18. Also look for up to 50 percent of the nitrogen in a slow-release form.

At times you will also want to apply individual nutrients. Often when a green-up is needed after you have already used a full lawn fertilizer, a nitrogen-only source may be needed. Various organic and man-made products could be used to feed the lawn with just nitrogen. Some soil recommendations suggest extra potassium is needed. Again, this nutrient can be supplied to bring the soil nutrient level up to what is needed to produce a good lawn. Check Table 3.2 for these nutrient-containing products.

When to Feed

Gardeners get lawn-feeding fever in spring and fall. Perhaps television commercials encourage these feedings that coax residents outside with their spreaders. These are also the two times of the year when lawns can make the best growth. After a long, sometimes quite cold winter, all grasses are ready for a good feeding. Often they have a yellowish appearance and the growth is rather slow. Just one spring feeding seems to bring them back to life, with warm temperatures and a good watering.

Unless you have the results of a soil test telling you otherwise, this is the time for a complete fertilizer application. Again, the general rule is a product with high nitrogen, little or no phosphorus, and medium to high levels of potassium. If iron deficiencies are a common problem, you may want to add considerable iron, usually at 1 percent or higher. Fall is another good time to feed lawns in a similar manner.

Other feedings are really up to you. Most likely the centipedegrass lawn will not really care, as it's not a high user of fertilizer. Bermudagrass and zoysiagrass lawns will want much more fertilizer, and seashore paspalum likes light but frequent feedings. The St. Augustinegrass and bahiagrass lawns only need fertilizer if they are on the yellow side or if you want a lot more growth. Many can be fed with a nitrogen-only fertilizer. Usually this is the one nutrient that is missing in the soil as you head into the summer season. Just choose one of the nitrogen-only sources. If it's in a totally soluble form, apply it at the rate of a half pound per 1,000 square feet of turf or, if in a slow-release form, up to one pound per 1,000 square feet. This is a good time to use products containing sludge and other natural organic fertilizers that slowly break down to release nutrients.

Still, most of us would like to have some type of schedule. Fertilizer programs for the major lawn types can be found in Tables 3.1a, b, and c. This will get you started on a good care program, depending on your location within the state. There are feeding schedules for three levels of maintenance. Most people will be happy with the results from the low to medium levels.

Weed-and-Feed

Each spring, gardeners have two lawn care chores on their minds—giving the turf a good feeding and controlling the weeds. Products that contain both a fertilizer and a weed killer are sold under the category "weed-and-feed." These prepackaged products are certainly a convenient way to provide the nutrients that lawns need and control some weeds.

Notice the phrase is control *some* weeds. Many gardeners believe these products are going to make all the weeds go away, and they are sure to be disappointed. Most weed-and-feed products just control the broadleaf types. A few also control germinating seeds. They also must be used specifically as

Different levels of fertilizer maintenance will achieve different results, and require varying amounts of work. Choose a program that suits your lifestyle and expectations.

instructed on the label to be effective. Some have to be applied to moist grass and weeds, while others must be watered into the ground. Warning: Read the label and be sure you have the proper product for your lawn type.

Another major factor in using a weed-and-feed is to make sure you apply it correctly. This means using the correct spreader setting or carefully figuring out the area to be treated and applying the correct amount. Failure to apply the correct amount over the designated area of lawn will result in less than anticipated weed control. It's best to use drop spreaders so you know exactly where the herbicide portion of the product is going. Most weed-and-feed products clearly recommend against use near trees or shrubs.

Some weeds are tough and will require a follow-up herbicide application in about a month or so. Usually this second treatment should be performed with a liquid form of the same herbicide found in the weed-and-feed.

Organic Versus Man-Made

We hear a lot about the value of using organic fertilizers. Certainly there is a lot of confusion about the term "organic." Organic fertilizers simply are those that contain the element carbon. Most often labels listing organic content are referring to the nitrogen in the fertilizer. These fertilizers can be naturally occurring, as manures and sludges, or are man-made products such as urea.

Here is the real question: Does the turf care? The answer is no. Grasses use nitrogen in one of two forms: nitrate nitrogen or ammoniacal nitrogen. Microorganisms must convert all organic sources of nitrogen to one of these forms before the plants can use them. Generally, organic nitrogen sources are considered to be slowly available, while man-made products are often quickly available. A mix of both is often used to formulate fertilizers.

When selecting fertilizers, also think of the man-made slow-release products. When you read the label be sure to look for urea formaldehyde, isobutylidine diurea (IBDU), sulfur-coated urea, or polymer-coated urea products listed as the nitrogen nutrient sources. All of these have slow-release, man-made qualities built into the fertilizer, which helps prevent pollution and maximizes your fertilizer dollar. You may also find slow-release, natural products such as sewage sludge, manure, and blood meal as all or part of the fertilizer. Modern fertilizer products usually state how much of the nitrogen is in a slow-release form. It's probably best to use products with up to 50 percent in the slow-release form.

Winterizing Your Lawn

Florida lawns usually get at least one major fall feeding sometime between September and November. This may be all the winterizing your lawn needs. If you find the lawn is a bit yellow, you might add what garden centers market as a winterizer. It's usually low in nitrogen, low in phosphorus, and has a medium to high level of potassium. There is a general feeling that potassium applied during the fall and about thirty days before the first frost can toughen the lawn. You can provide the potassium and green the lawn just a little with one of these winterizer type fertilizers.

Don't be surprised if lawn care companies suggest a potassium-only fertilizer application to lawns around late October or early November. It won't harm the grass and may give the same winter protection as a winterizer, especially if you have been following a good care program. University of Florida recommendations also suggest one pound of potassium per 1,000 square feet of turf be applied, especially to bahiagrass and St. Augustinegrass lawns. This can be supplied by 1.6 pounds of muriate of potash or two pounds of potassium sulfate. Irrigate the lawn after applying the treatment.

Reading the Fertilizer Bag

How often do you read a fertilizer label? Most gardeners don't get past the analysis and the weight of the bag. Some are also curious about the fertilizer settings, often listed, which can help make the chores a little easier. If you have never taken a few moments to read the label, now is the time.

Each product lists the analysis, which could be a 16-4-8, 15-5-15, or similar set of numbers. The first number is the nitrogen, the second the phosphorus, and the third the potassium. Each represents the percent of these nutrients in the bag. For example, the 16-4-8 product contains 16 percent nitrogen (NO_3 or NH_4), 4 percent phosphorus (P_2O_5), and 8 percent potassium (K_2O). If you add the numbers together you get a total of 28 percent nutrients, which equates to twenty-eight pounds of these macronutrients in 100 pounds of the fertilizer. If the fertilizer contains all three of these nutrients, it's called a complete fertilizer. If one of the nutrients is missing, as with a 15-0-15 product, it's called an incomplete fertilizer.

The label also lists the source of the nutrients for each of the fertilizer elements, and how much of the nitrogen is in water-soluble and water-insoluble forms. The soluble nitrogen forms are readily available to feed your plants, but

Fertilizing

also rapidly leach from the soil. Modern fertilizers list their slow-release features and the percentages of nutrients in this form. You will also find a list of the micronutrients and the sources.

How Much to Apply

Perhaps the easiest way to determine the amount of a lawn fertilizer needed is to follow the label recommendations. They typically make it fairly easy, suggesting spreader settings or pounds needed to feed an area of turf. This may be all you need to know if you are using standard brand-name products. But what if you just purchase a fertilizer by analysis or nutrient source? How do you know how much to apply?

Modern fertilizer recommendations are based on the nitrogen applied to the turf. Usually recommendations call for one pound of nitrogen for each 1,000 square feet of lawn. But fertilizers are not just nitrogen. There are often other nutrients in the bag and filler, too. No matter what the fertilizer might be, if it's a type that can be used for lawns, there is an easy way to determine the amount of fertilizer needed to supply one pound of nitrogen: Simply divide the percentage of nitrogen into 100.

100 divided by the % nitrogen in the bag = the amount of fertilizer for each 1,000 square feet

For example, if you had a 16-4-8 analysis fertilizer, divide 100 by 16. What do you get? The answer is 6.25, which equals 6.25 pounds of fertilizer. This is the amount needed to supply one pound of nitrogen. It should be scattered over every 1,000 square feet of turf.

For 4,000 square feet of lawn, you would still use 6.25 pounds of fertilizer for every 1,000 square feet. To determine the amount needed per feeding, multiple 6.25 by 4. So you come up with 25 pounds needed per feeding.

New recommendations suggest applying a full pound of nitrogen to the turf only when half of this nutrient is in a slow-release form. We do this to be environmentally friendly. To follow this recommendation you have to learn how much of the nitrogen in the bag is slow release. If it's about half, apply the full one pound rate. If all or much of the nitrogen is quick release, consider using less. Florida recommendations suggest using a half pound of nitrogen when the nitrogen source is all quick-release fertilizer. Consult Table 3.3 for nutrient sources and the rates that might be used with your lawn.

49

How to Apply

Just tossing out handfuls of fertilizer is never the best way to feed a lawn. While it's certainly done from time to time, it is surely a way to burn turf and get uneven fertilizer applications. We have all seen those green spots, and the yellow areas that have been missed, in lawns when fertilizing has been done a handful at a time. The best way to fertilize a lawn is with a spreader. Garden centers and hardware stores offer two types of spreaders: drop type and rotary.

Drop-type spreaders uniformly spread the fertilizer under the hopper as it moves across the lawn. You can count on an even fertilizer application right where you want the product. Each pass of the spreader must abut the previous application to avoid skipped areas in the feedings. Drop-type spreaders come in assorted sizes but one just a few feet wide is probably best for home use. This is a great spreader to use where you want precision applications, especially with weed-and-feed type products.

Rotary spreaders, also called cyclone and centrifugal spreaders, distribute the fertilizer by whirling it out over a larger area. Higher amounts of the fertilizer usually drop close to the spreader, so it's necessary to overlap passes just a little for uniform application. Due to the distribution pattern, there are less likely to be areas that do not receive at least some fertilizer. Also larger areas of lawn can be covered in a shorter period of time. Rotary spreaders toss the fertil-

Fertilize your lawn wisely. Have your soil tested, carefully evaluate the health of your turfgrass, and take into account weather conditions before developing a fertilization schedule.

izer out over large areas, which reduces their precision and may make them less suitable for weed-and-feed applications, unless the equipment is properly calibrated and the products can be applied where they won't affect nearby plantings.

Fertilizers are typically applied to a dry lawn. If the grass is wet, many nutrients attach to the leaves and can cause burn. Usually it's best to spread the fertilizer and then apply about a quarter to a half of an inch of water to move the fertilizer into the root zone. One exception is weed-and-feed products formulated for application to moist lawns; these are commonly the types with postemergence herbicides. Read the label to make sure you are using these products properly.

Some fertilizers can also be applied in a liquid form. It's important to make sure the fertilizer is spread over the area suggested on the label and with the proper amount of water. These are usually quick-release products and should be applied at the half pound of nitrogen rates.

Calibrating Fertilizer Spreaders

Applying the proper amount of any product is a major problem in caring for lawns. Apply too much and you could burn the turf. If you don't use enough, then you may not obtain the desired greening, weed control, or pest control. Many granular products come with spreader settings on the label. But perhaps your spreader is not listed or maybe your spreader is a little older and not working like it used to. What can you do?

You probably should check the spreader's efficiency at least once a season. It's not a difficult task but does take a little time, an open area, and a scale that weighs ounces up to a few pounds. Before doing the test, it's best to spread a piece of plastic over your driveway so you can collect the fertilizer afterward.

To test a drop-type spreader, measure the width of the spreader and divide 100 by this number. This will give you the length of a test area needed for 100 square feet of treatment. Add fertilizer to the spreader and practice making passes over the test area.

Start the test with plastic free of fertilizer granules and begin at the lowest setting. Make a pass and then collect the granules and weigh the amount. Make several tests each with a higher setting and weigh and record the amounts each time.

Next determine the amount of fertilizer needed for 1,000 square feet of lawn and divide it by ten. For example, if you are applying a 16-4-8 fertilizer, you would be applying 6.25 pounds of fertilizer (remember, you would divide

100 by sixteen to get this number). Divide this amount by ten again to give the amount of fertilizer needed for 100 square feet. In this case you would need 0.625 pounds, or ten ounces.

From your tests determine the setting that is closest to the amount of product that should be applied, and use this setting for the spreader. Similar tests can be made to determine the proper settings for granular weed control products, insecticides, or fungicides. You may have to make more test runs to find the best setting, and test each different granular product separately.

Finding the best setting for a rotary spreader takes a little more room. Often a driveway is best, with a long, wide sheet of plastic. Fill the spreader with the fertilizer to be tested. Open the spreader about halfway and make a pass over the plastic to determine the width of application. Measure the width of the area over which the granules were distributed. Use about two-thirds of this width as the effective treatment width.

For our example, let's say the effective treatment width is ten feet. Now determine how much of the fertilizer product being used should be applied to 1,000 square feet. If you use a 15-5-15 fertilizer, it's about 6.6 pounds. Divide this by ten to get the amount of fertilizer for each 100 square feet of test area—in this example, it would be 0.66 pounds.

Now measure out a test strip of plastic ten feet wide and fifty feet long. This equals 500 square feet and will require 3.3 pounds of fertilizer (5 × 0.66 pounds). Fill the spreader with a specific amount of the fertilizer, say ten pounds, and make a run down the test strip at a low setting. Weigh out the fertilizer left in the spreader at the end of the test. Let's say you have seven pounds left of the original ten. This means you applied three pounds of fertilizer over the test area.

Make several additional tests until you can determine a setting that provides the proper amount of fertilizer to be applied. In this case, you would only have to raise the spreader setting just a little. You can run similar tests with other granular products to determine proper settings.

Special Feedings

Most gardeners want that good green look from a lawn, but they may not get it solely from the regular feedings. And continually applying a complete fertilizer or nitrogen-only product can produce a lot of clippings and overgrowth of runners. It also increases thatch buildup in lawns.

Read the fertilizer bag carefully before making an application to your lawn.

Sometimes lawns need just an iron application. Grasses such as bahiagrass and centipedegrass frequently suffer from an iron deficiency. This is typical in soils that either lack iron or have a higher soil pH. Also iron may be present in the soil but not be available because of growing conditions. Iron deficiencies are not abnormal, especially during the late winter or early spring months. Often gardeners apply a spring feeding and the yellowing just gets worst, because the turf needed an iron-only application.

Iron can be supplied in liquid or granular form. Garden centers usually offer iron sulfate, chelated iron, or natural iron sources. When it is applied at the label rate, the results can be dramatic. Re-greening usually takes place in just a matter of days.

Iron can also be used as a nitrogen fertilizer substitute during the summer months. Several evenly spaced applications during the summer can produce the green look without all the growth. This may be a way of conserving fertilizer and protecting the environment at the same time. Note that iron products can stain walkways, streets, and buildings. They should be swept or washed from these areas before they cause the familiar brown marks.

Clean Up Time

Do you feel that crunching under your feet and have you noticed the spots on the sidewalk? That's where some of the fertilizer particles landed after you fed the lawn. Fertilizer application anywhere but the lawn is not going to help the turf and it may lead to permanent stains on the concrete, and ground water pollution since the nutrients could end up in lakes and drinking water.

It's just a good idea to clean up after fertilizing the lawn. Sweep or blow the fertilizer particles off the sidewalks and out of the roadways onto your turf, so you can get maximum use of the fertilizer and the best value for your fertilizer dollars. After all, not much grass grows on your sidewalks or in the roadways!

Mowing

Chapter Four

> **Mow Often**
>
> **Mow High**
>
> **Use a Sharp Blade**
>
> **Mow in Alternating Directions**
>
> **Recycle Clippings**
>
> **Invest in an Earth-Friendly Mower**
>
> **Consider a Mulching Mower or Blade**
>
> **Push, Don't Ride**

Mowing is not a chore that everyone loves. But gardeners do seem to take a lot of pride in a manicured lawn and some find that freshly cut turf has a certain pleasing fragrance. We must not truly mind mowing or we wouldn't have as much lawn!

Like it or not, there is plenty of mowing to do in Florida. Even during the winter months many lawns are very active and must occasionally be mowed. Also mowing does help control weeds, so it usually should be done regularly even if you are not cutting much of the grass.

Mow Often

All grass types are usually active year-round except bahiagrass. Bahiagrass responds to day length and seems to stop growing around the end of October. It won't really begin growth again until mid-March. The rest of the turf types respond more to temperature. If the weather is warm, mowing may be needed at any time, but growth does slow a bit during the cooler months.

How often you mow is up to you. Most gardeners find once a week adequate. During the rainy season of June through September the grass may grow faster than you would like and you may need to mow every five days. And if you want to keep a manicured look with the finer-bladed grasses, more frequent mowing is preferred.

In general, if the turf produces new growth equal to one-third the desired height it's time to mow. For example, if you want to keep your St. Augustinegrass lawn at three inches and it grows to four inches, it's time to mow. Removing more than one-third of the leaf blade can stress turfgrass, make lots of clippings, and result in yellowing of the grass.

So letting the grass grow very tall and then mowing is a mistake, but so is cutting it too short. A close cut may make you feel good and delay the next mowing, but it really hurts the grass. Leaf blades are food-manufacturing centers. The more leaf blade, within reason, the more food the grass can produce. So if you cut the turf too short, you shut down the food-producing centers and the grass begins to decline. Mowing too close also reduces the size of the root system.

Mow, Then Measure

There are several ways to adjust the height of the mower blade. One approach is to set the mower on a sidewalk or driveway and then measure the height of the mower blade above the concrete or similar surface. This gives you an approximate mowing height, but it's not that accurate.

Perhaps the best way to adjust the mowing height is on the lawn. If you want a high mowing height, position the deck of the mower so that it's set well above the grass, then make a cut across the lawn. Measure the height of the cut grass blades to see if this is the proper height. If not, adjust the mower

Mowing grass high encourages deeper root systems, which are better able to withstand environmental stresses.

again by raising or lowering the wheels of a push mower or the deck of a riding mower to achieve the proper height. Make as many adjustments as needed until you get the proper height. You might have to experiment with several test areas in various sections of the lawn and use an average height.

Lawns often have dips and ridges that can affect mowing. Try to keep the blade high enough to avoid scalping these sections of the lawn. If areas of the lawn are too uneven, some fill soil or even resodding may be needed to develop a uniform turf. Lawns also develop sponginess over time and to maintain the desired mowing height you may need to adjust the height of the mower throughout the growing season, and even from one year to the next.

Mow High

A general rule is to mow the grass at the highest recommended height for the lawn type. People are often misled to believe cutting the grass closely reduces the frequency of mowing. What it really does is destroy the grass. As mentioned, too close a cutting reduces the lawn's ability to produce the needed food for growth. The grass blades are food-manufacturing units that absorb sunlight and turn nutrients from the air, water, and fertilizers into new plant portions. If cut too close, the turf loses vigor and cannot compete with weeds, insects, and diseases, and the grass gradually declines.

Each turf type has its own preferred mowing height, normally a range. Check in Chapter Six for the proper mowing height for your lawn. For example, the standard St. Augustinegrass varieties can be mowed to between three and four inches. For most lawns it's probably best to choose the highest height. University studies show that the higher the leaf blade the deeper the root system, which increases the water and nutrients the grass can absorb. Also, because of an improved root system, the turf is more resistant to insects, nematodes, and disease. Most modern mowers have a restricted height for safety reasons. Usually setting the mower at the maximum height gives the best level for St. Augustinegrass and bahiagrass lawns. Most mowers can be adjusted for the very close cuts needed for finer-bladed turf types.

Avoid letting the grass get too tall before mowing. Try to have the lawn mowed when you go on vacation or don't have time to tend to it yourself. Drastically lowering the height of the grass blades stresses the lawn and can make it more susceptible to sunscald and pest problems. If the grass grows too tall between cuttings, gradually reduce the height over a series of mowings.

Also do not raise and lower the mower blade with the season. For some reason gardeners believe the grass is better cut at different heights throughout the year, but this is not the case. Where possible, select one height and keep your mower at this height year-round. Remember, the higher the better, especially since a high cut is a water conservation practice, and even improves shade tolerance of the grass.

Sharp Blades Are Better

Sharp mower blades give the best-looking lawns. Check the grass after each mowing for signs of torn ends that indicate a dull lawn mower blade. You can usually spot the effects of a dull lawn mower blade just an hour or two after the mowing job—the surface of the lawn will have a brown tinge.

Dull lawn mower blades not only make the turf look bad, but could cause some pest problems. Diseases love the ragged ends where the tissue is damaged and open to fungal growth. A good sharp cut heals rapidly to prevent the organisms from entering. Ragged cuts also lose more moisture, which stresses the turf.

Vary your mowing patterns in order to prevent soil compaction. If you mow in one direction one week, then mow perpendicular or diagonal to that the next week.

How often you need to sharpen the blade depends on the turf type, the size of the lawn, and frequency of mowing. Plus, in Florida you often have the sand factor. If the lawns are open and coarse in texture, more sand may be sucked up into the mower to dull the blade. And don't forget, some lawns are just more difficult to mow. A tough-bladed bahiagrass lawn can dull a mower blade much faster than a soft St. Augustinegrass lawn.

Besides inspecting the grass edges, inspect the blade itself. When the blade develops a rounded edge and nicks from hitting debris, it's time to have it sharpened. During an active mowing season with the average-sized lawn, the blade needs sharpening about once a month.

A really good idea is to keep a second blade or set of blades sharp, handy, and ready for use. When it comes time to remove the blade from a rotary mower, follow the instructions in the owner's manual. In general, you will need to disconnect the spark plug and use a clamp to hold the blade still while the bolt is loosened. Follow all safety recommendations suggested in the manual. You can sharpen the blade yourself with a file or grinder. But to be honest, it's not a fun job, and mower shops do the sharpening quickly and economically. Many will sharpen blades while you wait. Reel mowers need special sharpening techniques, best done by a professional.

Rotary vs. Reel Mowers

Rotary (powered)	*Reel (manual)*
Initial low cost	Low yearly cost (no gas or oil)
Easy to maneuver	Good for grasses needing lower cuts
Basic maintenance	Only maintenance is sharpening
Ideal for uneven surfaces	blades and bedding knife
No raking (with mulching	Smooth cut (better on level ground)
mowers)	No emissions

Don't Get Stuck in a Rut

We have all seen them—lawns with deep ruts across the surface. Where do these ruts come from? This is simply where the wheels of the mower run every time the lawn is cut. These gardeners are stuck in a rut and it shows. The lawns are not as attractive and the soil could become compacted in those areas.

Don't get stuck in a rut! Try to take a different path through the turf at each mowing. Maybe mow a square pattern one time and a diagonal pattern another. You might be surprised that the grass may take on a different look just by changing the mowing routine. You often see the patterns on ball fields—they're made by changing the mowing routes. If you do have ruts, just changing your mowing habits will gradually help them disappear.

To Bag or Not to Bag

Forget bagging your grass unless you have a very good reason. Leaving the clippings on the lawn keeps the yard waste at home and avoids adding it to the landfill. Also the grass clippings contain nutrients the turf can use. Some studies suggest that returning the clippings to the lawn can provide nutrients equal to one feeding a year. So don't allow this free lawn food to be hauled away to the dump.

Many gardeners fear that the lawn clippings contribute to the thatch layer or can suffocate the grass. If you are giving your lawn good care with proper watering and feeding, the lawn's clippings should not be excessive nor cause problems. And the leaf blade is mainly water. It shrivels and falls down between the remaining leaf portions in a matter of hours after cutting. Leaf and stem portions falling to the ground and decomposing are normal parts of the grass growth cycle.

If you want to speed the grass decomposition process and perhaps have a neater-looking lawn, you might consider using a mulching mower. This type of mower grinds up the leaf blades by keeping them within the mower longer, so they will be cut into smaller pieces. Mulching mowers work well as long as the grass is cut frequently. If the grass is too tall, the mower bogs down and is not able to cut the blade portions into the smaller pieces. In most cases, however, mowing the lawn frequently to return the small pieces of grass to the ground is more important than what type of mower you use.

Sometimes you may get behind in mowing because of a vacation or frequent rains. The grass may grow too rapidly a week or two during the summer and become exceptionally high. When this happens, you are going to have lots of clippings, so it is probably best to catch the clippings or rake them up after the mowing. With some lawn diseases such as rust, you may also want to catch the clippings for a few mowings to prevent spreading the spores among the healthy turf. In general, when the clippings are caught or raked, use them in the compost pile. They decompose very quickly and can be returned to the garden soil or used as mulch after the composting process is complete. If the lawn has a problem such as rust, dispose of the clippings rather than compost them.

Thatch—The Real Story

If you are over-watering and overfeeding the lawn, you are going to get thatch and lots of it. Thatch is the accumulation of grass blades, runners, and other grass parts just above the soil line. All lawns have some thatch from normal grass decline. Thatch can become very thick, however, if lawns are growing too rapidly. It can harbor pests, affect the activity of pesticides, prevent water and air movement into the soil, restrict desirable root growth, and produce a spongy lawn.

Some thatch is desirable. Generally half an inch is considered acceptable. It acts as a mulch to hold in moisture to prevent rapid drying of the soil. It also returns nutrients to the ground for turf growth. All lawns have some thatch near the ground surface; it can look like loose decomposing leaf blades and stems or a finer peat-moss-like material.

Gardeners should realize, however, that dead grass blades that accumulate on the surface of the turf at the end of winter is not thatch. These are winter-damaged grass parts that can become thatch over time. These brown leaf blades can be raked from the lawn or left to be hidden by new spring growth. Also the overgrowth from St. Augustinegrass lawns, consisting of loose run-

Grass with
Thatch Layer

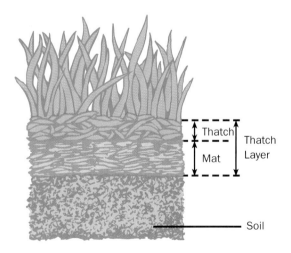

Thatch

Mat

Thatch Layer

Soil

ners above the surface of the soil, is not thatch—but it is a problem. This over-growth produces a very spongy lawn that is difficult to mow and manage. Like excessive thatch, this is usually caused by overfeeding and over-watering.

Thatch becomes a problem when it develops a thick layer that affects turf growth. Most professionals believe that a thatch layer of one inch or more is a problem. Optimally you will recognize the beginnings of a thatch problem before you get a one-inch or deeper thatch layer. Most home lawns do not have a thatch problem, but gardeners are often convinced they do. Just cut a slice of your turf and take a look. If you see the accumulation of a thick thatch layer, then you need to take some action.

Remember that some thatch is normal, but if it's accumulating rapidly you need to adjust your care program. Make sure you are not over-watering or over-fertilizing the turf. Maintaining the lawn with a low to medium feeding program and watering only when the grass indicates it is beginning to dry usually keeps thatch to a minimum. Also check the soil acidity. Proper pH promotes the best grass growth and the activity of microorganisms that decompose the grass portions forming the thatch layer.

Thatch can be mechanically removed from lawns but it can be a devastating process. Rental centers usually have vertical mowers that cut into the turf and lift the thatch out. If necessary, thatch removal is normally done during the growing season, from spring through early summer. Select a vertical mower made for your lawn type or adjust the blades to the proper spacing. Coarse turf types such as bahiagrass and St. Augustinegrass need a vertical blade spacing of three inches. Finer turf types like bermudagrass and zoysiagrass need a one- to two-inch spacing and use a two- to three-inch spacing for centipedegrass. The blades are usually adjusted to cut down to the soil line and a pass is made across the lawn. Then check the amount of thatch removed and damage to the turf. A second pass can be made as needed. Making too many passes with centipedegrass and St. Augustinegrass lawns can cause the complete removal of the grass, so use caution.

After vertical mowing is complete, remove the thatch brought to the surface from the lawn. Also mow the lawn slightly closer than usual. Keep the turf moist as if starting a new lawn to prevent drying of the exposed runners and roots. One week after treatment, apply fertilizer to encourage new growth. Remember that thatch removal can be devastating to lawns, so make sure you really have a thatch problem before considering a treatment. Also try to use cultural controls to minimize thatch accumulation. Your best bet is to maintain proper watering and feeding and to check pH levels to minimize thatch accumulation.

Core Aeration to Relieve Soil Compaction

Most Florida soils in home landscapes are composed of sand. So why does it need aeration? It might not unless it becomes compacted during neighborhood football games, is difficult to wet, has a nematode problem, or has developed a thatch problem. Healthy Florida lawns that consist of moist, loose, pest-free sands gain little benefit from aeration. But if your turf is not growing well because of problems that aeration can help, you might give it a try.

Rental centers have aerators for home lawn use. One type puts a hole in the ground with a spike. It lets air into the soil but can compact the ground at the same time. The best aerator pushes a tube into the ground and pulls out a plug of soil. This leaves an open hole where loose soil can fill in to prevent compaction. The plugs of soil are then left on the surface of the ground to disintegrate with the next mowing or watering. In either case, the equipment is simply run across the surface of the turf much like a mower. This is best done when the grass is making new growth during the spring through early fall months. Hand aerators consist of tubes that can be pushed into the ground and may be used for small areas of turf. They usually would be too much work, however, to treat an entire lawn.

Aeration allows water, fertilizer, and new roots to penetrate deeper into the ground. It is best done when the soil is slightly moist. Try to time the aeration with a scheduled watering and feeding to encourage a wetting of hard-to-wet soils. This also provides conditions that promote better root growth into the soil.

Topdressing

The high-maintenance turf of golf courses, athletic fields, and similar areas often receive a topdressing as a way of reducing thatch. The added soil increases microbial activity to encourage decomposition of the accumulating organic matter. This is probably not a technique most homeowners are going to use regularly, although they could find it an answer to spongy turf. Again, spongy grass usually results from too much water or fertilizer, or from improper soil pH. You must also address these problems to help prevent the spongy growth.

When topdressing is used for thatch control or sponginess, it involves adding soil or sand to the surface of the lawn. Preferably the topdressing material should be the same or similar to the soil type where the grass is growing. It should also be free of weeds, insects, diseases, and nematodes. Some garden centers are now marketing soil specifically for topdressing lawns, although many gardeners simply use pest-free sand. An application of sand or soil should not be greater than a half inch. If you need a thicker layer to take the sponginess out of the lawn, make repeat applications throughout the growing season. Frequent but light applications are the best way to keep thatch under control if needed in higher maintenance lawns. Thicker topdressing layers may be used to fill depressions but to avoid a decline of the grass, should not cover the turf.

Recommended Rate for Topdressing per 1,000 Square Feet of Lawn Area:

Topdressing Thickness (Inches)	Cubic Volume (Cubic Feet)	(Cubic Yards)
1/8	10.42	0.39
1/4	20.83	0.77
5/16	26.04	0.96
3/8	31.25	1.16
1/2	41.67	1.54
5/8	52.08	1.93
3/4	62.50	2.31
1	83.30	3.09

Getting Ready for Winter

Does a Florida lawn ever really get ready for winter? Yes, but not in the same way as in a more northern climate. Quite often the grass makes constant growth during the late fall and winter season. And if your lawn is bahiagrass, which does slow growth drastically during the shorter days, you will have weeds to contend with throughout the cooler months. Just mowing the weeds that grow in any lawn can help the turf better survive the cooler months. Other lawns can be active and need constant mowing. Resist any urge to adjust the height of the cut just because it's winter. Remember that it's best to keep the mower blade at the same level year-round to encourage good growth.

Wise Mower Maintenance

Change oil seasonally
Recycle oil
Replace spark plug and air filter seasonally
Fill the gasoline tank only three-quarters full,
    allowing for heat expansion
Avoid gasoline spills
Keep blades sharp and decks clean of clippings
Review owner's manual

Taking good care of your lawn, for its optimum health and appearance, also means taking care of your mower.

As with our northern neighbors, in late fall and winter some tree and shrub leaf accumulation will be left on the lawns. The fallen foliage is best removed to prevent smothering the grass. You can rake it up, or, if you don't have too much, shred it during a normal mowing and bag it. If the leaves are collected, use them as a mulch or add them to the compost pile. When leaves are extra heavy, as from a big oak tree, rake and remove them from the lawn, and don't try mowing over them.

Protect the Environment and Get in Shape

Mowers are getting better but most are still gas-powered engines that produce exhaust and pollute the air. You can help your mower operate at peak performance by doing regular maintenance, including cleaning and replacing the spark plug and air filter as needed. Check the owner's manual to determine the intervals for all needed service, including oil changes.

There are also alternatives to gas-powered equipment. Electric mowers operate on house current with an extension cord or use rechargeable batteries. These are very user-friendly and often appropriate for the smaller home lawns. Gardeners can also use the push reel-type of mower, which could be a good way to get your exercise—but do check with your doctor before you undertake this somewhat strenuous gardening activity.

End of Season Care for Power Mowers

Run engine until all fuel is gone
While engine is warm, drain oil and replace with fresh oil
Clean deck
Lubricate appropriate parts
Remove battery and charge it before storage
Enjoy the break from mowing!

Low Maintenance Lawn Ideas

Chapter Five

Create Curves Not Corners

Divide and Conquer

Group Trees Together

Avoid Berms

Convert High Traffic Areas

Avoid Narrow Bands of Turf

Create Mowing Strips

Consider Lawn Alternatives

Lawnscaping

Florida residents now have to carefully plan how much lawn they really need. In the past, much of the landscape was turf. But in the interest of conserving water and creating low-maintenance landscapes, we all need to decide the best use for home turf. Just as you decide how much of the landscape will be trees, shrubs, and flowers, take time to decide how much lawn to plant. We call this "lawnscaping."

You might want lots of lawn just because you like a long green open vista, although in smaller landscapes you might not have a lot of room for that. But most gardeners do like to have open spaces, which can be created with turf. Also you need room for family activities such as tossing the ball around, playing badminton, and pitching horseshoes. Then there are times you just want to throw a toy for the dog to retrieve. These are all fun activities best done on grass.

Establish lawns where they are accessible to other family areas such as the patio, walkways, and gardens. And consider maintenance: If the area is going to be difficult to mow or seldom used, it might be better devoted to other plants. Keep the lawn a size that you can conveniently maintain. Don't be a slave to your turf—plan and plant only what you can care for in a reasonable time. And restrict turf to the good growing areas. There is no use planting in areas where the grass is not going to succeed.

Creating curved edges on your landscape beds makes for easier and quicker mowing.

Curves, Not Corners

Good landscapes have lots of curves. This makes for easy maintenance. They are often called the "lines of beauty." Simply put, curves are pleasing to the eye. There are no boxy lines and abrupt endings as with squarish designs. Yes, smooth, gently sweeping curves are what you want. But avoid too many undulating lines that make for a lot more work.

You will soon learn that curves are very pleasing to look at and easy to maintain. Your mower just naturally moves along the outline of the curves. You don't have to stop and back up and then make special cuts as you often have to do with corners. Nice curves also soften the harshness of some architectural features, such as walls, arbors, and gazebos, and help tie garden areas together, giving unity to the overall landscape design.

Trying to visualize the bed lines is often difficult, but it becomes easy with just a simple trick. Stretch a hose or long extension cord out to form the shape of the landscape edge. If it's not what you like, move it until you have the look you want and mark where the line is, with flags, stakes, spray paint, or by digging the line with a shovel. Then till the ground and fill the beds or establish the grass according to your design.

Divide and Conquer

Think of your outdoor living area as an extension of your home. You have rooms in the home, so why not outdoors? In any one yard you may have a play area, rest area, and work area. Like rooms inside the home, they are often separate and partially or totally hidden from one another. With good landscaping, you can screen out bad views and reduce noise. Walking from one area of the landscape to another should be a pleasing experience with lots to see, sounds to hear, and fragrances to entice the nose. Plants help you create the walls of the room and assist you in decorating. Divide up your landscape on paper or in your mind and then decide how plants can help form your outdoor living areas. When you do, consider the lawn areas your carpets. They could be the foot ticklers you love to walk on with your bare feet. Others will just be good cushiony paths that allow for your family activities and provide the element that unites all aspects of the landscape.

Trees Mean Shade

You cannot have trees without shade. Some trees are very open and others are quite dense. As a general rule, if you have more than 25 percent shade, it becomes difficult to grow grass. Many gardeners lament that grass was used under the trees because now they have bare ground. Don't forget that as trees grow older, they also get bigger and begin to compete more and more with the turf. You can often thin out the trees and that helps some, but often the grass still does not grow as well. And when trees get big, it's often impossible to reestablish turf in the shady spots. But why is that?

You have to remember that trees, too, have roots. And as the trees get larger, the root system fills the ground under the spread of the limbs and beyond. Have you ever tried to dig a hole under an oak tree? If it's tough for you, just think how difficult it is for the grass roots. Some gardeners try adding soil over the tree roots, but because roots need oxygen, you cannot add too much or you suffocate the trees and they decline. Nor can you dig out too many of the roots or the trees may die. In these tough areas, you may need something besides grass.

Group Trees Together with Mulch

Having one of this and one of that creates a confusing landscape when you are dealing with flower beds, shrub plantings, or trees. Plants scattered throughout the landscape also make care a lot more difficult. You have to mow around the trunks, being mindful not to damage the plants. Most plantings should also be mulched and many gardeners like to add some flowers or ground covers. All landscapes look a lot better if the tree and shrub plantings are connected in small to large beds.

Often it's just a matter of creating bed lines to connect the plantings. This is another good time to use the garden hose or an extension cord to outline the edges of the beds. Building beds may eliminate some areas of grass, but ties the plantings together, creating what landscape architects call unity in the design. Create the beds by first using a general non-selective weed control product that allows replanting after the unwanted vegetation declines. Then, as the unwanted vegetation dies, spread a mulch layer to complete the bed.

Gardeners have many mulches from which to choose. University of Florida studies show all organic mulches help to conserve moisture and keep a uniform soil temperature. People do have their preferences and usually select barks rather than compost and yard waste mulch. Remember that organic mulches are temporary and the two- to four-inch layers created near trees and shrubs have to be renewed throughout the year. It's just a matter of adding more mulch to bring the layer up to its original level. Many gardeners are also choosing decorative rock and rubber products as mulches for the landscape.

Bed areas are also a good spot to add ground covers, shrubs, and even pots of flowers. The areas under the trees can become accent features with lots of color, a birdbath, or wind chimes. The mulched spots could become rest areas, with a bench set along a walkway where you can stop for a while and enjoy the wildlife that may be visiting the landscape.

Ground Covers Instead of Grass

Sometimes you have to give up and admit you cannot grow grass. The area may just be too shady. Grass may have grown in that spot at one time, but the trees are now bigger so there is more root competition. Also some areas are just too small to devote to turf, and some are too difficult to maintain. In such cases you might want something a bit more permanent, such as an ornamental ground cover.

These are plants that may need occasional trimming but, once established, can usually exist with minimal care. Planting ornamental ground covers is a great way to reduce maintenance. They consist of native and introduced plants that have attractive, often evergreen, foliage and even beautiful flowers. Many are very competitive and grow well with tree roots in the shade or filtered sun. Others can take full sun locations and many are

Lily Turf

Purple Heart

Lantana

Perennial ground covers can be used instead of turfgrass in shady places or high traffic areas. Some good choices are ajuga, lily turf, lantana, purple heart, Mexican heather, and mondo grass.

drought tolerant. In a water-conscientious Florida, ground covers are becoming a common replacement for turf where grass is not needed or desired. Choices for sun or shade include Asiatic jasmine, caladiums, and wedelia. In deep shade you might choose cast iron plant, peacock ginger, English ivy, Algerian ivy, or bromeliads. But there are many more great ground covers to choose from.

Ground covers are not a complete replacement for grass. Usually they cannot tolerate foot traffic. One solution is to use pavers or mulches where you have family activities, or create pathways through the ground cover plantings. You will need to do some trimming, too. Ground covers do just what the name implies—cover the ground—and many can be very vigorous. Often you will have to edge beds and keep the vining types away from the trunks of trees. Some also have insect and disease problems, but they are usually minor, if a problem at all.

Moss, Lichens, and Algae—Friend or Foe?

Most Florida gardeners won't see much moss except in the damp shady spots of the landscape. The dry-land dwellers may have lichens, one of which is called deer moss, in the natural areas. And wherever you have lots of moisture and limited air movement, there could be algae. Mosses and lichens are interesting, tidy plants that could substitute for turf and act as a ground cover. Of the three, algae is the least desirable and often gardeners work to control it.

Few Florida gardeners ever try to establish moss or lichens in their gardens. These are best left to grow on their own, as the conditions needed for success are very specific. If moss does not have enough moisture year-round, it is not going to survive, and if lichens are disturbed much or kept too moist, they are going to decline. Perhaps it's best to use these lower forms of plants in the natural areas where they exist, or create gardens that can include them in the design.

Berms—Oh, My!

Oh, yes, even Florida landscapes can have berms, especially in the rolling lands and hilly sites. Some berms are also created for special effects, to hide views and create the mountain-like feel of more northern landscapes. Berms are also created in areas with poor water drainage to allow plantings and permit the use of septic systems. Some berms are part of swales used to move water from one area of the landscape to another.

Grass can be used to cover berms but it should be a drought-tolerant variety or have available irrigation for the dry times. If berms become dry they are difficult to wet. Florida sands, when dry, often repel moisture. When the soil does dry, only light, frequent watering can be used to moisten the ground. Some gardeners use wetting agents to help rewet the soils or they aerate the soil just before watering. Without adequate moisture, the grass can decline and erosion can become a problem. Where berms cannot be watered and grass is needed, gardeners might consider bahiagrass or other drought-tolerant selections.

Many berms can be covered with ornamental ground covers but you need tough, durable types. Where water is limited, Asiatic jasmine or confederate jasmine might be a good selection. It sends out a very dense root system to hold the soil together and can grow in sunny or shady locations. For a native plant in the sunny areas, gardeners might choose the mimosa or sensitive plant that hugs the ground. Where ground covers are needed, first control the unwanted vegetation covering the berm with a nonselective weed control product that allows replanting. Mow and then plant the ground cover through the remaining brown vegetation. The declining grass and weeds will help hold the soil together until the ground cover becomes established.

There are other ways to deal with berms, including terracing the sites and stabilizing the soil with pavers and rocks. Gardeners have to decide which will give the best look and be the most practical for their landscape and pocketbooks.

High Traffic Sites

Footpaths used by you, your neighbors, or the family pets are never a good spot for turf. Sure, we do have some tough grass varieties, but they will still have trouble with the constant foot traffic. You also have to deal with the compaction of the soil. Areas of compacted soils drain poorly and are good places for weeds to become established. Turf on athletic fields receives frequent aeration or is even replaced from time to time. But that's probably not something you want to do on a regular basis.

It is true that every landscape needs paths from one area of the design to another. Often the direct route is not the best path. A walkway should take you past interesting sites and often avoid the turf altogether. Plan pathways early in the landscape design. Create paths that lead from the patio to rest areas, other garden sites, and the work areas of the landscape. A constantly used path should be made of something besides grass.

Often gardeners use mulch for the walkways. It's inexpensive and quick. Other options include flagstones, pre-cast pavers, wood, bricks, concrete, and similar materials. If you decide to use concrete, make it interesting. In each section embed the imprint of a plant or make some artistic designs. One Florida gardener created a palm walkway with the imprint of a palm frond in every poured section. For fun you can create concrete stepping-stones decorated by family members. First make a firm, level foundation of sand—which is not very difficult to do in Florida—and then add the materials needed to form the walkway. If you use mulches or loose stones, you might consider first putting down a landscape fabric to help control weeds and keep the materials from sinking into the sand.

Walkways may be very formal or include plants as part of the design. Some gardeners use low growing ground covers such as mint or mondo grass between the pavers or bricked sections. These may need some trimming from time to time, but help take away the formality of the design.

In high traffic areas, install walkways to avoid compacting the soil. Make the paths a part of the overall garden design by creating curves, using an attractive surface material, and leading visitors past interesting views.

Narrow Sections of Turf— Accidents Waiting to Happen

Possibly gardeners haven't thought about it much, but small sections of turf require a lot of work. You have to keep them moist, fertilize them, and then get the mower running to do the cutting. Some of these small partial lawns are on a bank or at the edge of a shrub border. Many of these areas are also near the street where it could be hazardous to do the mowing. The mower could slip off the curb or you could head out into traffic without looking. Have you noticed that street-side spots of St. Augustinegrass are also the first to dry out and get chinch bug problems? Most likely planting something else besides turf in these locations is preferable.

A small spot in an urban landscape could be a site of a new garden. Maybe you would like to add roses or just a bed of annuals. These do take some work but add lots of color. For lower maintenance but similar appeal, add a bed of wildflowers or maybe some easy-to-maintain perennials. Ground covers are also great additions. A bed of low-maintenance liriope, Asiatic jasmine, or wedelia may help these landscapes. Once established, they need very little water or fertilizer.

Where a small section of turf is at the edge of an existing landscape planting, consider making the bed just a little bigger. You could add a few more shrubs or maybe a ground cover. In fact, all you may have to do is add a little more mulch to replace the turf.

Edging or Mowing Strips

Nothing makes a landscape look better than a nice edge where beds of flowers or shrubs meet the turf. But gardeners often just let the grass run wild and it gets into the plantings. This means lots of work pulling the unwanted turf out, often disturbing the flowers, shrubs, and ground covers. It also

Mowing Strips Along Landscape Beds

makes mowing more difficult as it's difficult to tell what is turf and what is ornamental.

There must be a better way, and there is: creating a more formal edging at the point where the grass meets the beds. One possible solution is to create a flat surface at the edge of the beds using "mowing strips" available from garden centers. They are installed between the grass and the ornamental plantings to provide a flat, even surface for the wheels of the mower. If you want to use a more traditional surface, consider using bricks, pavers, and flagstones to create your own mowing strips.

Another way to keep the grass at bay is to use a shovel to form a sharp edge to the beds. As the edge is created, leave a shallow trough to backfill with mulch or similar materials, to bring the bed edge up to the level of the turf. This also provides an area between the turf and the ornamental plantings where the wheels of the mower can travel.

Edges for ornamental plantings can also be created with upright plastic, wood, or fabric materials available at garden centers. Gardeners also turn bricks and stones on edge and some invest in concrete borders. These rise a few inches above the turf and do not provide a surface for the wheels of a mower. You have to decide if they are appropriate for your landscape design. Grass eventually grows over or under the barriers and the edges will need some maintenance.

Most Florida grasses are invasive. Only bahiagrass grows rather slowly, but it too can send out long runners during the damp, hot weather. Periodically the shoots must be controlled by edging near the mowing strips, shovel-formed edges, or barrier materials. In most cases, using a mechanical edger, string trimmer, or shovel to limit the growth of the turf is best. If done regularly, it's not very time-consuming or difficult. Application of an herbicide is not recommended unless the turf has entered the nearby beds. Such treatments applied to the turf runners often cause the grass to die back at least partially into the lawn, creating unsightly dead areas that may allow weeds to become established. However, there are grass-specific herbicides commercially available that are safe to use over the tops of ornamentals. Read the label for tolerant species.

Turf Varieties

Chapter Six

Warm-Season Grasses Best for Florida

Match Grass to Growing Area and Soil Type

Consider Personal Preferences

Be Aware of Time Needed for Maintenance

Research Suitable Varieties

Look for Improved Pest-Resistant Selections

Selection of Grasses

In the past it's been pretty easy to select a grass—either St. Augustinegrass or bahiagrass. In fact, most homeowners did not have a choice, but received what came with the house or what the community mandated. Today gardeners are looking beyond the norm. They want the best grass.

What has really complicated grass selection is Florida's water problems. When water flowed freely and at minimal cost, perhaps St. Augustinegrass was an easy choice. Some gardeners watered often and kept that nice green lush lawn. It looked good but it may have not been the healthiest turf. We have since learned that lawns kept on the lean but still attractive side are more resistant to pests and deeper rooted. They also may be more cold hardy and are certainly a lot less work.

Bahiagrass was known as the least expensive lawn. This turf has been cut out of pastures for years, which helped reduce costs. It also was easy to install. Sod set on the home site and given minimal care almost always survived. It's not a bad-looking lawn, has low-maintenance requirements, resists abuse from family activities, and is drought tolerant. But to a new Florida resident it's a little coarse and has an open growth habit.

Florida residents have started to look for new turf types, often egged on by flashy ads that appear to offer a "so-easy-to-grow" grass. Just put in the plugs or toss out the seeds, the ads say, and you can have a carefree lawn. Nothing comes that easy, but maybe the other grasses are still worth a look.

Some of these grasses are drought tolerant and have that Northern lawn look. You know—the foot ticklers. It's always tempting to try something new, but you have to check out all the features. As one person says, if it sounds too good to be true, it probably is. But each grass has its own advantages and disadvantages. One may be drought tolerant but has more pests or may need additional feedings. So how are you going to decide which grass to grow?

First determine how much time you want to spend with your lawn. At a minimum in Florida you are probably going to have to mow once a week, April through October. Even during the cooler fall and winter months, you may need to cut the grass. Then decide how often you want to feed the lawn, water, and check for pests. Do you want to learn how to apply chemicals and will you have to install an irrigation system? Is your soil adequate or will you have to make adjustments?

Start your quest for a new home lawn by making comparisons. Sometimes choosing the turf is easy. If you have lots of shade, it's probably going to be a St. Augustinegrass variety. But here, too, you have to be selective because only certain varieties have the lower light tolerance you need. Also if you live near the seashore, only a few turf types are really saltwater tolerant.

Some gardeners start their selection by looking at the leaf types. They want a grass like the one they grew up with. Many want a fine-bladed grass. Take a look: You can choose from bermudagrass, zoysiagrass, and seashore paspalum. You can take your shoes off and feel the grass blades on your toes. But is one of these the turf you want? They are very drought tolerant and can withstand lots of family activity. Now take a look at some other features such as mowing, feeding, and frequency of pests. Is one of these really the right grass for you? It might be.

Most people just need to do their homework and make a good comparison of the advantages and disadvantages of each turf type. When you have a grass in mind, look at the varieties. Check for pest resistance. Some may have fewer bugs or be more tolerant of cultural problems. Also check out the cost. Can you use seed to start your lawn or will you have to install sod? There is a lot to think about when selecting the home turf.

Tricky Ads

Every year there are ads for "sure-to-grow" grasses. These turf varieties must certainly grow as well as claimed somewhere, but often not in

Florida. Many grasses sold as seed are quick-cover turf varieties. These germinate rapidly to cover the ground and then decline under the harsh Florida conditions. Growing conditions are a bit different here than other regions. The fescues, bluegrasses, and even the ryegrasses are not permanent turf types for Florida. Check out any ad with your county Extension agent or a nearby garden center. Usually the grasses you need can be purchased locally.

Some ads also promise a grass that is easy to install, needs little care, and creates the perfect lawn. Sounds great, but you had better check this out, too. Often the grass grows well in other soils but has a more difficult time in Florida sands. It usually takes more water and fertilizer to grow any grass here, and requires more mowing. Again, ask your local experts about the grasses mentioned in the ads. It's probably best to get your turf locally rather than ordering seed or plugs through the mail. You can get more turf for your money when you don't have to pay for shipping, and generally the plugs are bigger and greener when purchased at local garden centers or turf dealers.

Shop for Good Seed

Old seed left over from last year is not likely to have the best germination. Also you probably don't know the storage conditions that might affect the growth of the grass even if it does germinate. When shopping for seed, look for a recent test date. The more recent the test, the better. Luckily Florida does have a good seed law, and test dates and germination information are required on every bag.

Look for a germination of at least 85 percent. The higher the percentage, the better to ensure a good stand of grass. Also try to select a seed that contains 90 percent or more of the grass variety you are purchasing. Look for the amount of other items in the seed. Ideally you should find seed with very little weed content and inert matter, no more than 10 percent.

Good Sod and Plugs, Too

Gardeners usually obtain turfgrass grown as plugs from garden centers. The practice of offering plugs started in the 1980s. It was a convenient way to market turf, and residents could easily purchase just one or numerous trays of the plugs, take them home, and plant them. If you buy plugs, make sure the grass looks fresh. It should be bright green and each plug should be full of shoots. Avoid trays of plugs with yellow grass or plugs that have become rootbound. These are often slower to grow into the surrounding soil after planting. Many that have been in the trays for an extended period of time also have runners shared between plugs and they can be difficult to separate.

The fresher the sod the better. You want the greenest and fullest sections of sod available. Less-attractive sod is only acceptable after cold weather browns the leaf blades, and only for a matter of a few weeks after the severe cold. If you pick up the sod at a garden center, reject yellow sod or sod that has been at the garden center for several days. Don't be surprised when the sod has just a little soil. Most sod is cut with about three-fourths of an inch of soil. One trick to getting good sod is to find out when the sod is delivered to the garden center and be there shortly after the truck arrives. Also check the sod for weeds. Reject any sod with unfamiliar things growing in it, especially other grasses and sedges. Get to know these major groups of weeds.

Guidelines for Good Quality Seed, Sod, and Plugs

Seed

Recent test date

85% or more germination

90% or more seed of appropriate grass

10% or less weed seed and inert matter

Sod	**Plugs**
Green and filled in	*Green and fresh looking*
Not yellow	*Not yellow*
Recent delivery	*Not rootbound*
No weeds	

When ordering sod, try to have it arrive the day of installation. You want fresh sod cut the day of delivery if at all possible. During the summer, sod should be laid within forty-eight hours of being cut from the fields. Sod sitting on a pallet for a longer time begins to heat up, deteriorate, and decline. If the sod is delivered and you are not ready for installation, have it set in a shady spot to help reduce the decline. Refuse sod that is weedy. When sections are being laid, discard ones with even a few weeds. Crabgrass, wild bermudagrass (also called common bermudagrass), and sedge can come with sod from even the best fields. Most sod in Florida is sold "Buyer Beware." That means you have to take responsibility for making sure you receive a good product. Most sod is a quality product, but be alert to even a few sections that might not meet your standards for good grass.

There are many turfgrass options available. When choosing a grass for your lawn, consider your regional conditions, your particular site, availability at local stores, personal preferences in grass texture and appearance, anticipated use of the lawn, maintenance requirements, and pest resistance.

Table 6.1
Turfgrass Comparisons

Characteristic	Bahia	Bermuda	Carpet	Centipede
Growing Height	3–4 inches	$1/2$–$1^1/_2$ inches	$1^1/_2$–2 inches	$1^1/_2$–2 inches
Soil pH	5.5–6.5	5.5–7.5	5.0–5.5	5.0–6.5
Drought Tolerance	Excellent	Excellent	Very Poor	Fair
Salt Tolerance	Poor	Good	Poor	Poor
Shade Tolerance	Poor	Poor	Poor to Fair	Fair
Heat Tolerance	Excellent	Excellent	Excellent	Excellent
Cold Tolerance	Excellent	Good	Poor	Good
Cold Hardiness Zones	8–11	8–11	8–11	8–9
Wear Tolerance	Good	Excellent	Poor	Poor
Spreading Rate	Medium	Rapid	Medium	Medium
Color	Medium Green	Dark Green	Bright Green	Light Green
Texture	Coarse to Medium	Fine to Coarse	Coarse	Medium

Characteristics	Seashore Paspalum	St. Augustine	Zoysia
Growing Height	$1^1/_2$–2 inches	3–4 inches	1–2 inches
Soil pH	4–9	5.5–7.5	5.5–7.0
Drought Tolerance	Good	Fair	Excellent
Salt Tolerance	Excellent	Good to Excellent	Good
Shade Tolerance	Fair	Good	Fair
Heat Tolerance	Excellent	Excellent	Excellent
Cold Tolerance	Good	Poor to Good	Excellent
Cold Hardiness Zones	8–11	8–11	8–11
Wear Tolerance	Excellent	Fair	Excellent
Spreading Rate	Rapid	Rapid	Medium
Color	Dark Green	Dark Green	Dark Green
Texture	Fine	Coarse	Fine to Medium

Bahiagrass

Paspalum notatum

Bahiagrass may be the ideal turf for home landscapes because it is drought tolerant and free of most pests. It also needs minimal feedings, is economical to plant, and tolerates the neighborhood football game. So why doesn't everyone grow bahiagrass? For one thing, it's a fairly open-growing turf with wide leaf blades, giving the lawn a coarse look. Gardeners also object to the numerous seedheads that grow more than a foot tall, produced spring through late summer.

Bahiagrass was first introduced to Florida farmers from Brazil in 1914. The earliest selection, simply termed common bahiagrass, gives the poorest home turf with light green leaves, an open growth habit, and poor cold tolerance. Other selections followed that grow much more attractive home turf. 'Argentine' is considered the best, and has good leaf color, numerous leaf blades, and fewer seedheads. 'Pensacola' bahiagrass, as the name suggests, was discovered growing in Pensacola, Florida, and has a relatively narrow blade and numerous seedheads.

You probably won't find bahiagrass sod at local garden centers, but you can order it from landscapers and sod growers. Because of slower lateral growth, it is not offered as plugs. Bahiagrass can also be seeded to establish a new lawn between March and early September. Bahiagrass requires a lot of iron, and if iron is unavailable because of low supplies in the ground or cool seasonal temperatures, the grass can turn a bright yellow color in spring. Apply an iron-only product when the iron deficiency is noted.

Bahiagrass

Facts

Growing Height—3 to 4 inches

Mow When Grass Reaches—4 to 6 inches

Soil pH—5.5 to 6.5

Drought Tolerance—excellent

Salt Tolerance—poor

Tolerance of Partial Shade—poor

Heat Tolerance—excellent

Cold Tolerance—excellent

Cold Hardiness Zones—8 to 11

Wear Tolerance—good

Spreading Rate—medium

Color—medium green

Texture—coarse to medium

Planting Methods

Seeding Rate—7 to 10 pounds per 1,000 square feet (use scarified seed for best germination).

Best Seeding Time—March through early September

Germination Time—14 to 21 days

Sod—16 inches wide by 24 inches long. A pallet usually contains 400 square feet.

Best Time to Sod—February through October but can be installed year-round.

Advantages

Drought tolerant

Deep root system

Nematode tolerant

Wear resistant

Low maintenance

Relatively pest free

Disadvantages

Coarse, tough leaf blades

Open growth habit

Yellows easily because of lack of iron

Tall, numerous seedheads

Mole cricket is major pest

Primary Pests

Insects: Armyworm

Billbug

Mole Cricket

White Grub

Diseases: Brown Patch

Dollar Spot

Fairy Ring

Leaf Spot

Other: Armadillo

Moles

See the appendix for a list of cultivars.

Bermudagrass
(Wiregrass, Devilgrass)
Cynodon dactylon

Bermudagrass produces the foot-tickling lawn everyone would love to have but few have the time to care for. It's considered a high-maintenance grass needing frequent mowing, feeding, and pest control. For the best look, bermudagrass varieties should be cut every three to five days with a reel mower during periods of rapid growth, but a rotary mower can be used. It is drought tolerant if you can allow your green lawn to turn brown. To stay green, it needs as much water as any other turfgrass. Bermudagrass originated in Africa and was brought to the United States originally for pastures. Many varieties have since been selected or bred for use in home lawns, athletic fields, and golf courses. It is generally considered the grass of choice for a sports turf and is commonly found on putting greens throughout Florida.

Most attractive bermudagrass lawns require extensive care and should be considered carefully before selection for a home lawn. One variety developed by the University of Florida and Texas A&M University, named 'FloraTex', has a lower maintenance level and some tolerance to pests. Bermudagrass is a vigorously growing turf and can fill in quickly from plugs or sprigs. It does go dormant during the winter months in North Florida but rapidly re-greens with the return of warmer weather. In colder locations the grass may be over-seeded with ryegrass. In Central Florida the top is frequently browned by frost but new shoots push up in a matter of days. Common bermudagrass frequently invades other types of turf.

Bermudagrass

Facts

Growing Height—$1/2$ to $1^1/2$ inches

Mow When Grass Reaches—$3/4$ to 2 inches

Soil pH—5.5 to 7.5

Drought Tolerance—excellent

Salt Tolerance—good

Tolerance of Partial Shade—poor

Heat Tolerance—excellent

Cold Tolerance—good

Cold Hardiness Zones—8 to 11

Wear Tolerance—excellent

Spreading Rate—rapid

Color—dark green

Texture—fine to coarse

Planting Methods

Seeding Rate—hulled seed 1 to 2 pounds per 1,000 square feet, non-hulled seed 3 to 4 pounds per 1,000 square feet for new lawns.

Best Seeding Time—April to July

Germination—10 to 14 days

Vegetative Planting Rate—5 to 10 bushels of sprigs per 1,000 square feet for a 6 to 12 inch spacing. 30 to 50 square feet of sod per 1,000 square feet to make 2-inch plugs spaced 12 inches apart. Trays of plugs are also available. Sod 16 inches wide by 24 inches long. Divide total square footage of lawn by 400 to figure pallets of sod.

Best Vegetative Planting Time— March to October

Advantages

Grows throughout Florida

Wide pH range

Drought tolerant

Salt tolerant

Fine-textured grass

Excellent wear tolerance

Great for family activities

Good weed resistance

Spreads rapidly

Disadvantages

Limited shade tolerance

Susceptible to nematodes

Reel mower preferred

High maintenance

Many pests

Goes dormant in cooler regions

Primary Pests

Insects: Armyworm, Billbug, Cutworm, Grass Scale, Ground Pearl, Mite, Mole Cricket, Sod Webworm, White Grub

Diseases: Bermudagrass Decline, Brown Patch, Dollar Spot, Fairy Ring, Leaf Spot, Pythium Root Rot

Other: Armadillos, Moles, Nematodes

See the appendix for a list of cultivars.

Carpetgrass
(Flatgrass, Louisianagrass)
Axonopus affinis

Sometimes we use a grass for a special reason and that seems to be the case with carpetgrass. If you have wet, poorly drained soil, this is probably the grass for you. It has a shallow root system, so needs the abundant water that the damper areas provide. It has little or no drought tolerance. Carpetgrass also needs an acid soil in the pH 5.0 to 5.5 range. It's not a bad-looking turf, resembling St. Augustine with a wide leaf blade, which gives a coarse texture. It's considered a low-maintenance turf, but with a little care produces a good green color and dense growth.

Carpetgrass was introduced to the United States from the West Indies during the early 1800s and is sometimes found in the wild growing in the damper soils. It has a creeping growth habit that can be used to help establish a lawn from sprigs. It can also be seeded. One big problem for gardeners is the numerous seedheads that have to be mowed often during the summer. It also has poor nematode resistance and limited cold hardiness. The green turf turns brown with the first frost and slowly re-greens with the warmer weather. Carpetgrass does have some shade tolerance but is not as good as St. Augustinegrass in the lower light locations.

Carpetgrass

Facts

Growing Height—1½ to 2 inches

Mow When Grass Reaches—2 to 3 inches

Soil pH—5.0 to 5.5

Drought Tolerance—very poor

Salt Tolerance—poor

Tolerance of Partial Shade—poor to fair

Heat Tolerance—excellent

Cold Tolerance—poor

Cold Hardiness Zones—8 to 11

Wear Tolerance—poor

Spreading Rate—medium

Color—bright green

Texture—coarse

Planting Methods

Seeding —1 to 3 pounds per 1,000 square feet for new lawns.

Best Seeding Time—April to July

Germination Time—10 to 14 days

Vegetative Planting Rate—2 to 4 bushels of sprigs per 1,000 square feet for 6 to 12 inch spacing. 30 to 50 square feet of sod per 1,000 square feet to make 2-inch plugs spaced 12 inches apart. Sod 16 inches wide by 24 inches long. Divide total square footage of lawn by 400 to figure pallets of sod.

Best Vegetative Planting Time— April to August

Advantages

Grows in wet soil

Prefers acid soils

Low fertility needs

Can be started from seed

Disadvantages

Numerous seedheads during summer

Poor cold tolerance

Susceptible to nematodes

Primary Pests

Insects: Armyworm

Cutworm

White Grub

Mole Cricket

Sod Webworm

Diseases: Brown Patch

Dollar Spot

Leaf spot

Pythium

Other: Nematodes

Centipedegrass
(Chinagrass or Chinesegrass)
Eremochloa ophiuroides

Centipedegrass is often known as the poor man's turf because of its low fertility requirements. Actually if you overfeed this grass it could die. Plant explorer Frank N. Meyer brought it to the United States in 1916 as part of the seed he collected from China. Gardeners liked the lower, soil-hugging growth habit and the relatively medium textured leaf blade. Centipedegrass spreads by stolons and looks much like a miniature St. Augustinegrass. It's frequently found in the wild and may mix with other turf types kept under minimal maintenance programs. The grass has a good apple-green color and most gardeners would love a centipedegrass lawn, but it has some problems.

Possibly the biggest problem is nematodes, microscopic roundworms. One in particular, the ring nematode, seems to prefer centipedegrass and is not a major pest of other grasses. For this reason this turf has limited use in sandy soils, and is better adapted to growing conditions in northern portions of the state. Centipedegrass can also be slow to recover from cold winters and should not be fed too soon or until signs of natural greening occur. Centipedegrass lawns can be established from seed, sprigs, plugs, or sod. Because of the small size of the seed and slow germination time, seed is not the easiest way for home gardeners to establish this grass. Also centipedegrass may develop chlorosis, especially in alkaline soil, and need extra iron applications during the growing season.

Centipedegrass

Facts

Growing Height—1¹/₂ to 2 inches

Mow When Grass Reaches—2 to 3 inches

Soil pH—5.0 to 6.5

Drought Tolerance—fair

Salt Tolerance—poor

Tolerance of Partial Shade—fair

Heat Tolerance—excellent

Cold Tolerance—good

Cold Hardiness Zones—8 to 9

Wear Tolerance—poor

Spreading Rate—medium

Color—light green

Texture—medium

Advantages

Minimal maintenance

Grows in infertile soils

Medium-textured lawn

Disadvantages

Sensitive to salt

Slow to recover from cold

Iron deficiency in alkaline soils

Nematodes damage roots

Cannot withstand frequent foot traffic

Planting Methods

Seeding Rate—¹/₄ to 1 pound per 1,000 square feet for new lawns. Mix seed with sand or clean soil to distribute.

Best Seeding Time—April to July

Germination Time—14 to 21 days

Vegetative Planting Rate—2 to 4 bushels of sprigs per 1,000 square feet for 6 to 12 inch spacing. 100 to 150 square feet of sod per 1,000 square feet to make 2-inch plugs spaced 6 inches apart. Trays of plugs are also available. Sod 16 inches wide by 24 inches long. Divide total square footage of lawn by 400 to figure pallets of sod.

Best Vegetative Planting Time—April to August

Primary Pests

Insects:	Armyworm
	Cutworm
	Ground Pearl
	Mole Cricket
	Sod Webworm
	Spittlebug
	White Grub
Diseases:	Brown Patch
	Dollar Spot
	Fairy Ring
	Leaf Spot
Other:	Centipede Decline
	Nematodes

See the appendix for a list of cultivars.

Seashore Paspalum

Paspalum vaginatum

Gardeners needing a salt-tolerant grass should consider seashore paspalum. It's often found growing in salty water and near the ocean. The grass has been observed for years growing under conditions that have been unfavorable for other common turf types, but only recently received attention for possible use with lawns, recreation areas, and commercial sites. It's native to warmer portions of Africa and North and South America. Locally seashore paspalum first appeared when it was discarded from early ships entering U.S. ports, where it began to grow along the shorelines. Researchers have found that the turf has good drought tolerance and grows over a wide range of soil acidity. It can be mowed close and has a fine leaf blade to give that well-manicured turf look.

Several varieties were released during the 1990s. Success has been variable and many feel that good growth depends on the management provided. Turf specialists suggest that seashore paspalum grows best with frequent and light feedings. It's best to apply no more than a half pound of quick-release nitrogen per 1,000 square feet of turf at a single feeding, and up to one pound of nitrogen when 50 percent of this nutrient is supplied by a slow-release source. Seashore paspalum also benefits from extra potassium, and the rate of application should be at least equal to the nitrogen in the fertilizer analysis when a standard lawn fertilizer is used. Seashore paspalum can be irrigated with lower-quality recycled water or salty water now found in many coastal wells. The turf does need periodic flushing with water with a lower salt content—such as from rainfall—to prevent salt toxicity.

Seashore Paspalum

Facts

Growing Height—1 1/2 to 2 inches

Mow When Grass Reaches—2 to 2 1/2 inches

Soil pH—4 to 9

Drought Tolerance—good

Salt Tolerance—excellent

Tolerance of Partial Shade—fair

Heat Tolerance—excellent

Cold Tolerance—good

Cold Hardiness Zones—8 to 11

Wear Tolerance—excellent

Spreading Rate—rapid

Color—dark green

Texture—fine

Advantages

Saltwater tolerant

Fine-textured turf

Drought tolerant

Tolerates wide range of acidity

Tolerates wear

Disadvantages

Maintenance program critical

Prefers light but frequent feedings

Needs frequent mowing

Limited shade tolerance

Planting Methods

Vegetative Planting Rate—5 to 10 bushels of sprigs per 1,000 square feet for 6 to 12 inch spacing. 30 to 50 square feet of sod per 1,000 square feet to make 2-inch plugs for 6 to 12 inch spacing. Trays of plugs are also available. Sod 16 inches wide by 24 inches long. Divide the total square footage of lawn by 400 to figure pallets of sod.

Best Vegetative Planting Time— April to August

Primary Pests

Insects: Armyworm

Billbug

Cutworm

Mole Cricket

Sod Webworm

Spittlebug

White Grub

Diseases: Helminthosporium

Pythium

Take-all Root Rot

Other: Nematodes

See the appendix for a list of cultivars.

St. Augustinegrass
(Charlestongrass)
Stenotaphrum secundatum

St. Augustinegrass is the most widely planted home turf in Florida, having originated in the regions of the Gulf of Mexico, West Africa, and the Pacific Islands. In Florida one of its early uses reportedly was as a pasture grass. Gardeners like its dark green to blue-green color and dense growth habit. Most would rather not have the thick blades that give the lawn a coarse texture, but tolerate it because of the lower maintenance compared to the finer-bladed turf selections. St. Augustinegrass is the most shade tolerant of the grasses available for home planting. Numerous varieties are offered, and if the planting site has any shade, gardeners should select a type requiring lower light. Some of the more shade-tolerant selections include 'Amerishade', 'Bitterblue', 'Delmar', 'Palmetto', and 'Seville'. The grass spreads by stolons, which makes it easy to start new lawns by plugs. New lawns can also be started from sprigs and sod. Seed of St. Augustinegrass has been offered in the past, but has performed poorly.

St. Augustinegrass has a lower drought tolerance than other warm-season grasses. A deeply rooted St. Augustinegrass lawn can usually go a week without water in hot, dry times—and much longer during the cool winter months—before starting to decline. Gardeners should keep this grass on a low- to medium-care program to prevent excessive thatch and overgrowth of runners. Also vigorous growth during the summer usually encourages pests. St. Augustinegrass lawns need weekly mowings March through November. If the winters are warm, mowing every week or two may still be needed.

St. Augustinegrass

Facts

Growing Height—3 to 4 inches for standard selections; 2 to 2½ for semi-dwarfs

Mow When Grass Reaches—3 to 6 inches

Soil pH—5.5 to 7.5

Drought Tolerance—fair

Salt Tolerance—good to excellent

Tolerance of Partial Shade—good

Heat Tolerance—excellent

Cold Tolerance—poor to good

Cold Hardiness Zones—8 to 11

Wear Tolerance—fair

Spreading Rate—rapid

Color—dark green

Texture—coarse

Advantages

Good green color

Creates a dense lawn

Vigorous growth

Salt tolerant

Shade tolerant

Plugs and sod readily available

Disadvantages

Coarse texture

Prevalent pests

Some selections cold sensitive

Browns in northern locations

Susceptible to drought

Planting Methods

Seeding Rate—⅓ to ½ pound per 1,000 square feet. Few varieties.

Best Seeding Time—April to July

Germination Time—14 to 21 days

Vegetative Planting Rate—2 to 4 bushels of sprigs per 1,000 square feet for 6 to 12 inch spacing. 30 to 50 square feet of sod per 1,000 square feet to make 2-inch plugs for 6 to 12 inch spacing. Trays of plugs are also available. Sod 16 inches wide by 24 inches long. Divide the total square footage of lawn by 400 to figure pallets of sod.

Best Vegetative Planting Time— April to July for sprigs; year-round for plugs and sod in many areas.

Primary Pests

Insects:	Armyworm
	Chinch Bug
	Mole Cricket
	Sod Webworm
	Spittlebug
Diseases:	Brown Patch
	Fairy Ring
	Gray Leaf Spot
	Pythium Root Rot
	Rust
	Take-all Root Rot
Other:	Armadillo
	Moles
	Nematodes

See the appendix for a list of cultivars.

Zoysiagrass

Zoysia species

Zoysiagrass can produce a very attractive lawn that's drought tolerant and adaptable to most Florida soils. Most selections have some shade tolerance and resist damage from salt spray. A zoysiagrass lawn produces the fine-bladed, dense, manicured look people love for family activities and as a ground cover. In Florida zoysiagrass needs some maintenance—not as much as bermudagrass, but certainly more than St. Augustine. Having a nice lawn means more water, more fertilizer, and more mowing than gardeners are often led to believe. There is also a problem with nematodes, the microscopic roundworms that live in the soil and affect turf roots. If you want a zoysiagrass lawn, have a nematode test first to determine what you might need to do before installing the grass. Using a reel mower gives the best looking zoysiagrass lawn, but a sharp rotary mower also gives satisfactory results.

Various zoysiagrass species and varieties are available for Florida planting. These include *Zoysia japonica* (Japanese or Korean lawngrass or common zoysiagrass), available from seed; *Z. matrella* (Manilagrass), resembling bermudagrass; *Z. tenuifolia* (Korean velvetgrass or Mascarenegrass), which is the least hardy of the zoysias; and *Z. sinica* (seashore zoysiagrass, which should not be confused with seashore paspalum) available from seed. Most likely you won't be buying the species as such but one of the varietal selections. Zoysiagrass as seed, sod, or plugs can be purchased at your local garden center. Many gardeners order their zoysiagrass via mail and receive the small, almost thimble-sized plugs; plugs purchased locally are the full four square inches.

Zoysiagrass

Facts

Growing Height—1 to 2 inches

Mow When Grass Reaches—2 to 3 inches

Soil pH—5.5 to 7.0

Drought Tolerance—excellent

Salt Tolerance—good

Tolerance of Partial Shade—fair

Heat Tolerance—excellent

Cold Tolerance—excellent

Cold Hardiness Zones—8 to 11

Wear Tolerance—excellent

Spreading Rate—medium

Color—dark green

Texture—fine to medium

Planting Methods

Seeding Rate—2 to 4 pounds per 1,000 square feet for new lawns.

Best Seeding Time—April to July

Germination Time—14 to 21 days

Vegetative Planting Rate—2 to 4 bushels of sprigs per 1,000 square feet for 6 to 12 inch spacing. 100 to 150 square feet of sod per 1,000 square feet to make 2-inch plugs for 6-inch spacing. Trays of 4-inch plugs are also available. Sod 16 inches wide by 24 inches long. Divide the total square footage of lawn by 400 to figure pallets of sod.

Best Vegetative Planting Time— March to July

Advantages

Creates a dense, thin- to medium-bladed lawn

Drought tolerant

Resists wear

Grows in a wide range of soils

Disadvantages

High maintenance

Can develop a thatch problem

Can be slower growing

Will brown during the winter in cold locations

Nematode problems

Primary Pests

Insects:	Armyworm
	Billbug
	Cutworm
	Mole Cricket
	Sod Webworm
	White Grub
Diseases:	Brown Patch
	Dollar Spot
	Rust
Other:	Moles
	Nematodes

See the appendix for a list of cultivars.

Other Grass Varieties to Know

Buffalograss

Lots of gardeners have been looking for a native grass that can form a home lawn or recreational turf. Many have taken a look at buffalograss, *Buchloe dactyloides*, a native species found growing in the drier Great Plains areas of the United States. Interest always renews when Florida enters periods of extended drought. Buffalograss is a perennial, somewhat resembling bermudagrass, growing six to eight inches high. It spreads by stolons to form a fine- to medium-bladed turf with a blue-green color and open growth habit. It's found growing in the heavier native soils and seldom in sands. The grass has separate male and female flowers. Male flowers are produced at the tops of tall shoots often called "flags," and make the grass somewhat objectionable for home lawns. The less conspicuous female flowers develop nearer the ground. Some newer varieties are selections from the female types to avoid the taller seedheads.

Buffalograss is very drought tolerant and usually grows in locations that receive no more than ten to twenty-five inches of rainfall a year. During the dry weather it turns brown and goes dormant until the rains return. It has poor shade tolerance and little resistance to wear from foot traffic. In Florida it is also affected by excessive rains, often occurring during the summer season, which create a perfect environment for disease development, to which buffalograss is susceptible. The turf appears to be weakened and weeds often invade this slower-growing turf during damp weather.

Gardeners wanting to try buffalograss in dry sites can start the lawn from seed, sod, or plugs. Seed, which is actually burrs containing several seeds, is sown at the rate of one to five pounds per 1,000 square feet of new lawn. Deburred seed may also be available. The higher rates give better stands in a shorter period of time. Plugs are spaced six inches or more apart. Seed, plugs, and sod are all kept moist until the grass is established, and thereafter the grass needs little or no water and fertilizer. Too much of either is considered a major cause for the decline of buffalograss in Florida. The turf should be kept mowed to two to three inches high.

Ryegrass

Want a grass that you can just toss out, moisten, and watch it grow? We have one and it's ryegrass, *Lolium* species. The problem is that it cannot take the heat. Ryegrass of either annual (*L. multiflorum*) or perennial (*L. perenne*) species forms temporary lawns that survive well during the winter months. But no matter which ryegrass species you choose, it's going to decline during the early spring months as the weather warms since they are really cool-season grasses and should not be considered as permanent turfgrasses in Florida.

Ryegrass is ideal for overseeding and establishing a temporary lawn, and can be used to quickly fill in bare spots. Seed typically starts appearing at garden centers during the fall and continues to be available through spring. Usually the sooner it is sown after the arrival of cooler weather, the better it becomes established and the longer you can enjoy the bright green lawn. Seeding rates are usually about eight to ten pounds for every 1,000 square feet of lawn to be established, and ryegrass germinates in ten to fourteen days.

Even though ryegrass seed can just be tossed out, it's best sown on a prepared planting site. Till the soil, rake it smooth, and then scatter the seeds. After sowing, rake the seeds into the soil lightly and then moisten. As with all seedings, keeping the soil moist and feeding during the growing season, fall through early spring, is needed. Mow the turf at a height of between two and three inches.

Common Turfgrass Pests

Chapter Seven

> *Be Observant for Changes in Your Lawn*
>
> *Watch for Symptoms and Signs*
>
> *Gauge the Proper Time for Action*
>
> *Use a Process of Elimination to Identify the Problem*
>
> *Follow Good Management Practices*
>
> *Spot Treat if Possible*
>
> *Use Chemicals as a Last Resort*

All plants have pest problems and your turf is no exception. Many lawn experts believe that just good care will keep the pests away. It does help and your grass can become somewhat resistant to insects and diseases, but environmental factors often affect growth and make the grass more suscepti- ble to problems. Your lawn is constantly subjected to potential pests, but a healthy turf is resilient.

When the pests do sneak in you may have to take control. Early detection is the key to stopping pest problems before they cause major decline. Take frequent walks through the yard to spot symptoms of pest problems on all your plants, including the grass. You are the first line of defense against pest problems.

Take the time to identify the cause of the turf decline. Sometimes you have to get down on your hands and knees and part grass blades and dig in the soil to find the problem. Don't just reach for the pesticide or jump to con- clusions. Where needed, get help from a nearby garden center or your local University of Florida Extension office. The Extension agents and Master Gardeners usually need a square foot of sod with about an inch of soil, bor- dering the edge of the affected area and including both good and bad turf. This can help tell the story of what's wrong. Samples can also be shipped to the University of Florida pest identification labs and clinics for a more exten- sive diagnosis. There is usually a small charge for this service.

Sometimes the lawn problems are related to culture rather than to pests. Over-watering encourages root rot problems, growing the wrong turf variety in the shade leads to natural decline, and too much fertilizer can cause excessive vegetative growth that provides food for insects and diseases. Reviewing the proper care needed by your turf and putting it into practice can be a way of eliminating lawn problems. Also don't forget that your turf does have some helpers. Many beneficial insects, fungal and bacterial organisms, and similar natural controls are already at work. These include spiders, earwigs, and some diseases affecting the pests, which naturally live with the turf and soil.

When controls are needed, select the least toxic approach first. Sometimes pulling the weeds by hand is best. Maybe replacing a little sod is better than drenching with a fungicide. When pesticides are needed, look for natural products that won't deal a harsh blow to nature. If you must use synthetic products, try treating just the affected area of the lawn and a small buffer zone where the pests might be living. We can all reduce the use of pesticides to help protect the environment.

Diagnosing Pest Problems

Process of Elimination

Take a logical approach to your turf problems. Start by trying to figure out what you are really seeing. What are the symptoms and when did they first appear? What care have you provided and what does your turf actually need? Use the following list of questions to help you perform a diagnosis of the turf problems.

- *What are the specific symptoms? Be observant: Dig, pull, and look from different directions.*

- *Does the problem have a distinct pattern? Small independent circles? Large complete circle? Irregular appearance? Streaked appearance? Or no distinct shape at all?*

- *Is the problem in one spot or across the entire lawn?*

- *Do individual leaf blades have spots, distinctively shaped lesions, or streaked areas?*

- *Are the roots healthy, with abundant, white, fibrous roots? Or are they stunted, slimy, or chewed on? Do they have holes in them or are they an obvious color?*

- *How long has the problem been present?*

- *Did the problem seem to appear overnight? If so, when was the last time you were out in your lawn?*

- *What specific type of turfgrass is in your lawn?*

- *When was the last time you fertilized? What did you use and how much?*

- *Have you ever done a soil test? If so, when was the last time?*

- *Have you probed the area to see if your soil is hard or compacted?*

- *Did you check for buried foreign matter such as sand, nails, limestone, or other materials in the problem area?*

- *What is your mowing height?*

- *When did you last sharpen or change your mower blade?*

- *When and how often do you water?*

- *Is there a thatch layer? If so, how thick?*

- *What time of year is it: spring, summer, fall, or winter?*

- *Is there a drought occurring? High heat or humidity?*

- *Has there been an abundance of rainfall?*

- *Was there a recent light frost?*

- *What is your soil type or texture: sand, clay, silt, or loam?*

- *Have you ever topdressed your lawn? If so, with what?*

- *Does your soil drain well?*

- *Is the problem in shade, partial shade, or sun?*

- *Have you spilled something in that spot recently: oil, gas, fertilizer, paint cleaner, or something similar?*

- *Have you drained a swimming pool in that area?*

- *Is the area near a septic tank or sewer drainage lines?*

Troubleshooting Symptoms

Scenario 1 – Grass affected in more or less circular patterns:

Symptoms	Possible Causes
Center dead, yellowish edge of damaged area	Chinch Bugs
Yellowish-brown color with central area of healthy grass	Brown Patch
Grass yellow to brown and soil soft	Mole Crickets
Circles of dark green to yellow grass often with mushrooms	Fairy Ring
Spots grayish green to brown, leaves rolled, dry soil	Drought
Yellow, thin blades and weak roots	Excessive Water
Small bleached spots or circles	Dollar Spot
Circular areas of straw-brown grass	Dog Urine
Spots of yellow to brown grass	Chemical Damage (gas, herbicide, fertilizer)

Scenario 2 – Grass affected in irregular patterns:

Symptoms	Possible Causes
Slow decline, yellowish to brown area, restricted shallow roots, wilt	Nematodes
Slow decline, yellowish areas, grass thins out, stunted leaf blades	Bermudagrass Mites
Leaves dark then yellowish brown, leaves become slimy and mat together, white fungal growth	Pythium Blight
Yellowish spots with fuzzy orange lesions	Rust
Area fades in color or dries rapidly after watering	Soil Variation or Septic Tank
Grass thin, area wilts quickly, fertilizer doesn't seem to help	Root Competition
Tips of leaves bleached, then burned	Salt Burn
Weak, elongated growth, thinning lawn	Too Much Shade
Gradual decline of centipedegrass lawn	Centipedegrass Decline
Distinct lesions on foliage, turning yellow	Helminthosporium Leaf Spot
Yellowish or dead spots, grass pulls out easily	Billbugs
Grass blades chewed	Lawn Caterpillars

101

Yellowing and eventual browning of turf during summer and early fall	Take-all Root Rot
Damaged roots, dead areas, pearl-like insect in soil, mainly on centipedegrass	Ground Pearl
Leaf blades of St. Augustinegrass yellow with dark spots during summer and early fall	Gray Leaf Spot
Grass gray-green and shriveling to brown	Frost or Freeze Damage

Scenario 3 – Grass affected in streaked patterns:

Symptoms	**Possible Causes**
Grass bleached, yellow, brown, or dead	Chemical Burn (herbicide, fertilizer)
Grass yellow to brown in linear pattern	Buried Debris

Scenario 4 – Grass affected but in no particular pattern:

Symptoms	**Possible Causes**
Yellowish foliage especially on new growth or yellow between veins	Iron Deficiency or High pH
Gray leaf blades covered with gray, chalky, powdery growth	Slime Mold
Grass yellowish green on older leaves, eventually turning brown	Nitrogen Deficiency
Brown tips of leaf blades that are split or frayed	Dull Mower Blade
Grass spongy, runners exposed on surface growth	Thatch or Excessive Water and Fertilizer
Weeds present	Compaction or Poor Management
Stems and leaves turn reddish purple color	Reaction to Cold Temperature
Large ant mounds	Fire Ants
Frothy, spit-like substance on grass, blades turning yellow	Spittlebugs
Soil hard and scum, mold, or algae present	Soil Compaction, Poor Drainage, Too Much Shade
Roots cut off, dead areas in lawn, pulls up easily	White Grubs
Stems chewed off near soil surface, grass wilting and dead	Cutworms
Grass bleached or speckled, hopping insects	Leafhoppers
Raised soil in meandering tunnels	Moles
Holes in turf several inches deep and wide	Squirrels or Armadillos

Weeds

Weeds are just plants growing out of place. Many plants that you might call weeds, others think of as wildflowers. A petunia growing in a tomato patch may be a weed, as is a black-eyed Susan that has self-sowed into a bahiagrass lawn. But most gardeners trying to grow a lawn consider any plant that differs from the desired grass a weed. Creating a thick and vigorously growing turf can help keep the unwanted vegetation out of the grass—but not always. Some weeds are as competitive as the turf and just waiting for a small bare spot to open up in the grass to begin growth. It may be an area slightly damaged during family games or an area turned up by moles or digging squirrels. You don't have to do anything wrong to get weedy plants growing in your lawn. Weeds will find a way into your yard.

Quick action on your part can keep out weeds. Sometimes it's just a matter of adding a section of new sod to a bare spot. Or you might do the unthinkable and stoop over to pull the weeds. Getting an early start on weeds can prevent an infestation and the need to use chemical controls. You also need to prevent other pests such as insects and diseases from affecting the turf. While they may not totally kill the grass, they can create weak spots where weeds would love to grow.

You can become a weed expert in a short time. It's not necessary to know each weed by name, but you do need to be familiar with the types that could grow in your yard. By knowing the general types of weeds you are dealing with, a control can usually be determined. If further help is needed, you can drop a sample by your garden center or University of Florida Extension office for identification and control suggestions.

Broadleaf weeds are usually the easiest to spot in the lawn. They have large, oblong to rounded leaves with net-like veins. These may be some of the prettiest weeds, often producing colorful flowers that lead to seeds and the next generation. Broadleaf weeds can be annuals or perennials and grow year-round. These are probably the easiest to control. Some commonly noted broadleaf weeds include Brazil pusley, dollarweed, matchweed, and oxalis.

Grassy weeds may look somewhat like your turf. They normally have long, narrow to wide leaf blades with parallel veins and hollow stems. They flower and the inflorescence is usually held above the leaves, but is not very showy. Some, such as the sandburs, produce very sticky seedpods. Control of grassy weeds is more difficult because they usually resemble the turf you want to grow. Grassy weeds can be annuals or perennials and grow year-round, but most that are a real problem prefer warmer weather. Some grassy turf invaders include crabgrass, goosegrass, and Alexandergrass.

Sedges may be the most shiny, bright green, and upright-growing weeds in your lawn. Many gardeners mistake the sedges for grasses, so it's important that you learn the difference. Like the grasses, sedges have narrow leaves with parallel veins. But the sedges have stems that are triangular and solid. If you feel the stem of a flowering stalk from a sedge, the triangular shape is very obvious. The leaves also are formed in obvious clusters of three as they emerge from the ground. Sedges can be annuals or perennials. Most grow best during the warmer weather. There are a number of sedges in Florida, including the purple and yellow nutsedges, globe sedge, and green kyllinga.

Gardeners need a strategy when controlling weeds. The first part of the plan is to establish a vigorous, durable turf. This is easy if the lawn is given the care outlined previously. But still weeds can enter the lawn. Often the best control for any weed is digging or pulling it out of the grass. Once established, some are difficult to control. If necessary, chemicals can be applied to eliminate many weeds.

One type of product, selective herbicide, removes the weeds without major damage to the turf. Products are also available to prevent seed germination, called preemergence herbicides. Others remove the weeds after they are up and growing, called postemergence herbicides. Some products can do both. It's important that you read the label to know which weeds are controlled and the proper application procedure.

Another group of weed control products are the nonselective herbicides. These show no respect for your turf and kill both the weeds and the desired grass. They are most commonly used when renovating lawns or controlling spot infestations of weeds. Also read these labels very carefully.

All herbicides must be applied according to label instructions, including following the precautions listed. Remember, herbicides are meant to kill plants and could affect trees, shrubs, vegetables, and flowers growing near your turf. Take all precautions listed to protect your health. With many herbicides you need to wear protective clothing, including coverings over your body, gloves, and boots. You may also want to consider eye protection and a respirator. The label will have all the information for personal protection equipment (PPE).

To help you gain control of your unwanted vegetation problems, Florida weeds have been classified under three major categories. To apply the best control, you need to decide first whether you are dealing with a broadleaf weed, grassy weed, or sedge.

Cool-Season Annual Weeds

While most weeds in the more northern climates go dormant or may be killed by cold, some of the Florida weeds flourish during the cooler weather—and need some chilly weather to grow well. Only one grassy annual weed may be a problem and that is annual bluegrass. It's more of a problem with golf course grass than home lawns. But if you have the problem, preemergence herbicides can help prevent seed germination.

Chickweed   Carolina Geranium

Henbit   Asiatic Hawksbeard

Virginia Pepperweed   Heartleaf Drymary

Cudweed

Of major concern during the cooler months are the winter broadleaf annuals, including common chickweed, Carolina geranium, henbit, Asiatic hawksbeard, mustards, heartleaf drymary, and cudweed. Often these weeds and the winter-growing perennials create the need for cool-season mowings, because the more desirable grass may not be actively growing. These weeds may be nipped by freezes but usually grow back, and rapidly. Broadleaf winter annuals can be prevented by applications of a preemergence herbicide during the fall, and postemergence herbicide treatments as needed. Consult the product label for information on the weed type you are trying to control.

Annual sedges are normally not a cool-season landscape problem, because they grow poorly during cooler weather, but their growth may extend into the fall months. Most of the serious lawn problems are perennial sedges.

Warm-Season Annual Weeds

Alexandergrass

When the weather is warm to hot and there is adequate water, you can stand back and watch the weeds grow. Many are very competitive with the good turf and you need to be ready to take control. Some of the grassy weeds that begin growth in February or March as the weather warms are Alexandergrass, crabgrass, goosegrass, woods weed, and crowfootgrass. The main control is a dense turf and, where needed, a preemergence herbicide. Timing of the herbicide application is critical, especially for crabgrass, which begins growth when the day temperatures are 65 degrees or higher for four or more continuous days. This normally occurs in early February for South and Central Florida and the first week of March in North Florida. Missing these critical times may mean poor control of the crabgrass. Also preemergence herbicides usually have to be reapplied to

Crabgrass   Goosegrass

Woods Weed   Crowfootgrass

continue the control into the spring and summer months, following label instructions.

Broadleaf weeds are active, too. Some common warm-season annuals include carpetweed, chamberbitter, dayflower, doveweed, knotweed, and spurges. Some preemergence herbicides can help, but check the label carefully to determine if your weeds are affected. Most broadleaf weed control is done with postemergence products. These are applied soon after the weeds are observed germinating. It's best to control the weeds when they are small and most susceptible to the herbicide. Also try to apply these products during the cooler spring months to reduce possible injury to your turf. Many herbicides have restrictions on their use during the hotter months.

Annual and perennial sedges sprout seeds during the spring months. Some seed germination can be prevented by preemergence herbicides. Most sedges are controlled with postemergence products made specifically for sedges.

Carpetweed

Chamberbitter

Dayflower

Knotweed

Spotted Spurge

Year-Round Perennial Weeds

By far some of the worst weeds are the perennials. A majority of them start from seeds and, once growing, mature plants are a problem to control. Ironically, some of the grasses that grow to be weedy have relatives that are desirable turf-grasses. Common bermudagrass often invades or comes with St. Augustinegrass and bahiagrass turf. It is a real problem and best controlled by spot killing with a nonselective herbicide that allows replanting after the unwanted grass declines. Repeat applications may be needed as the weed regrows until it's eliminated. Because of the underground rhizomes, you are not going to dig this one out. Another perennial grass is bull paspalum, a clump-forming weed. This one is a bit easier to control by hand digging or spot killing just the clump.

Broadleaf perennials include dandelion, dollarweed, dichondra, Florida betony, Brazil pusley, matchweed, and yellow woodsorrel. Some can be prevented at the seed stage with preemergence herbicides, but most gardeners have to deal with them after they have become established. Check the label of postemergence herbicides to see which weeds are listed and apply as instructed. Many escape these products and have to be controlled by hand digging or a nonselective herbicide that allows replanting after the weeds decline.

Bermudagrass

Bull Paspalum

Dandelion

Most problem sedges are perennials. Some familiar types include yellow and purple nutsedge, globe yellow sedge, and green kyllinga. They have rhizomes at or below ground, with root systems that rapidly run through the turf. The nutsedges take their name from long-lasting underground storage structures that survive the tough times and start new growth. Most decline during the winter and begin growing in early spring. Luckily postemergence controls are available from your local garden center for the sedges. Just follow the label instructions. They can also be dug out of the lawn (but often sprout back from missed portions) or spot killed and new sod added.

Dollarweed

Dichondra

Florida Betony

Pusley

Matchweed

Yellow Woodsorrel

Weed-and-Feed Versus Liquids

Many gardeners like the convenience of weed-and-feed type products. The products contain both an herbicide and a fertilizer. Most often they are used during the late winter and early fall. Depending on the type of product, they may control the established weeds and prevent seed germination. Success with weed-and-feed products depends on following the directions carefully. Some products have to be applied to damp turf and others to dry grass and then watered in. If under-applied, weeds are not adequately controlled, and if too much is distributed, the turf could be damaged. Some gardeners also pick up the wrong bag of weed-and-feed or mix types if purchasing more than one bag. This can damage the turf. Check to make sure your grass type and weeds are listed on the label. Also note that many weed-and-feed products cannot be used under trees or near shrubs. Consult the label for proper use.

Granular herbicides are also available as preemergence products. These are often sold as crabgrass preventers, but they can control other grasses and some broadleaf weeds. They must be applied before the germination of the weed seeds, and repeat applications are often needed. Follow label instructions.

Yellow Nutsedge

Purple Nutsedge

Globe Yellow Sedge

Green Kyllinga

Some gardeners do not need to feed the lawn, or prefer applying liquid products. The same herbicides available in weed-and-feeds and herbicide-only granules are usually formulated into liquids. Often garden centers have an even wider selection of herbicides in liquid form. When applying liquids, use a sprayer. You can use a pump type or one that fits on the end of a hose. Read the mixing instructions carefully and make sure you distribute the recommended amount of herbicide over the proper square footage of turf. Treating with too little herbicide often results in poor weed control and using too much can damage the turf. Many of these products may also have restrictions about use near trees and shrubs.

Natural or Organic Herbicides

As with all pesticides, use the safest product first. This may be a natural herbicide, including soap-type products, vinegar, and cornmeal formulations. Most break down very quickly and some, such as the cornmeal, provide some nutrients for turf growth. Follow the label directions as carefully as you do when using a synthetic herbicide. Gardeners also hear of many home remedies for weed control. Some may be effective but could damage your plants. It's best to wait until university data suggest the product is effective and tests show what plants or animals could be affected. Also wear protective clothing, including gloves and boots, when using all pesticides.

Insects

We are no longer a spraying society. In fact, most gardeners would like to avoid applying pesticides, especially insecticides. It's just not a good idea to be applying insecticides everywhere in the landscape. If everyone in your neighborhood regularly applied pesticides to their lawn, that would be a lot of toxic products added to the environment.

Today the trend is to manage insect populations at levels that are least damaging to plant materials, including the turf. Some call this Integrated Pest Management, or IPM. It involves knowing your plants and the pests that could cause damage. It also includes monitoring the plants for these pests, and for beneficial insects and other natural controls. A good IPM program may also include pesticides when a pest has reached a predetermined threshold and other options have been exhausted.

Perhaps your best control for insects in the lawn starts with weekly walks through the landscape to check the turf. Keep a lookout for grass that may not be growing properly, the first yellow spots, and then eventual decline. The decline could have many causes and you do have to think about each. Lots of things look like insect damage, including dry turf, diseases, and nematodes. Actually, you should be checking for all these problems.

Get to know the good bugs. Not everything in the lawn is a pest. Spiders eat many lawn-damaging insects, as do earwigs, big-eyed bugs, and ant lions. If you see these beneficials at work, leave them be. And consider these helpers when thinking of spraying. Try to avoid damaging the beneficial insects and related organisms. A list of beneficial insects is on pages 130-131, identifying them and what harmful insects they eat.

All right, what do you do if you think you may have an insect problem? Don't just automatically spray. Get the proof you need to justify the use of an insecticide. Get down on your hands and knees and look for the culprit using one of the following techniques.

Seek and Find: Part the grass blades and look for the damaging pest. Chewing insects can often be seen feeding on the grass blades. Some are active during the night hours, so take a flashlight outdoors and track the critters down. Many insects are at or below the soil line. Pry apart the turf and be patient. In time chinch bugs can be seen scurrying about and spittlebugs moving between the leaf blades.

Flush Them Out: Some insects are good at hiding and you have to irritate them a little to bring them to the surface of the soil and within sight. Use a soap mixture at the rate of one and a half fluid ounces of a mild dish detergent in two gallons of water. Sprinkle this soapy mixture over four square feet of problem turf and watch the insects come to the surface. This is a good way to get a glimpse of chinch bugs, caterpillars, and mole crickets. You are also going to see lots of beneficial insects and worms coming to the surface. Learn which are the good guys and which need control.

Old Can Trick: Just about everyone has a coffee can, and it can be used to flush out chinch bugs. Remove both ends of the can and push one end of the can into the soil in a suspected chinch bug area of the lawn. The best spot is right on the edge, where good and bad turf meet. The cans do not push easily through St. Augustinegrass runners, so you may have to make some cuts around the outside of the can with a knife. When the bottom of the can is an inch or two in the soil, below the grass, fill it with water. If the chinch bugs are present, they will come floating to the surface of the water, possibly along with other insects.

Checking the Soil: At least one damaging insect lives in the soil most of its life. It's not floated out with water and soap very easily and you are not going to see it scurrying about. It is the grub. The best way to spot these critters is to get your hands dirty. Dig up a section of sod in the declining area of the lawn. Grubs are white and have a dark head. Several of these per square foot of turf usually indicates an infestation.

Get to know the pests that affect your turf, using the profiles that follow. When you spot some of the insects, determine if a control is needed. A few of the insects in the turf may be normal, and another factor could be causing the turf decline. You or a consultant needs to decide whether or not a pesticide application is necessary. Remember, you can always take a sample of the pest or the affected turf to your garden center or University of Florida Extension office to identify the pest and determine if a control is required.

When a pesticide is needed, select the least toxic product first. Various natural pest control products are appearing on the market to help with the control of lawn insects. One that has been around for a while is the *Bacillus thuringiensis* or Bt bacteria formulations to control lawn caterpillars. A beneficial nematode is also available to control mole crickets in commercial turf, and some naturally derived insecticides are becoming more available for lawn pests. As always, follow the label instructions.

Controlling turf pests does not necessarily mean spraying the entire lawn. Consider treating only the area affected plus a section of about five feet or so outside the damaged spots. This way you are just treating the infestation and leaving the unaffected areas free of the pesticide, and protecting the beneficial insects in the remaining section of the lawn that may have the pests under control.

Practicing good cultural care of the turf is another way to keep pests at bay. Chinch bugs and caterpillars love a lush, over-fed lawn and most pests can damage turf that is too closely cut or heat stressed. Review the care needed for your lawn type and see if the maintenance might be adjusted to improve its pest resistance.

Most Wanted List *(But Not in Your Lawn)*

Take a walk through the landscape, part the grass blades, and you are sure to find lots of creatures, including spiders, aphids, thrips, and sow bugs. Luckily most are not harmful to the turf and many are beneficial, feeding on organic matter and other pests. The descriptions that follow cover the insects most likely to damage your turf.

Armyworm
Spodoptera frugiperda

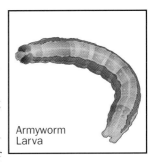

Armyworm Larva

Grass at Risk: Bahiagrass, bermudagrass, carpetgrass, centipedegrass, St. Augustinegrass, and zoysiagrass. All lawn grasses are potentially at risk during severe outbreaks.

Feeding Time: Spring through late fall. Some activity may occur during the winter in warmer areas of the state.

Overwinters As: All stages can be found year-round in warmer portions of Florida. Adults migrate to cooler sites during spring.

Detrimental Stage: Larvae feeding in the lawn.

Life Cycle: Overwintering adults lay eggs in clusters of up to several hundred on the turf and nearby plantings, providing the start of the next genera-

Armyworm Adult

tion. As with most insects, the life cycle is temperature dependent. Eggs can hatch in just a matter of days, producing the larval stage that feeds on the grass blades, usually for several weeks. Armyworms pupate in the soil, needing a week to a month before the adults emerge. Several generations may be observed throughout the year but armyworms are only sporadic pests of home turf.

Description: The caterpillars are green when small and become brown when fully grown, reaching one and a half inches in length. Older larval stages have light and dark stripes along their body. The mature larvae have an inverted "Y" on their heads. Adults are gray to brownish moths with a wingspan of up to one and a half inches, their wings marked with white spots. The eggs are greenish white and spherical, laid in masses. Pupae are reddish brown and mature in the soil.

Damage Symptoms and Signs: Chewing damage to leaves begins as nibbling on the surface of the grass blade when the larvae are small. As the larvae age and become bigger, they consume entire leaves and produce bare spots in lawns.

Scout and Count: Just a few caterpillars per square foot of lawn can produce severe damage. The larval stages feed mainly during the day and are usually easy to spot on the blades of the grass.

Management: Cultural practices such as proper mowing, feeding, and watering foster healthy grass and can help deter caterpillars. The presence of adults doesn't mean there will be a bad outbreak of larvae. Natural predators, parasites, disease, and environmental conditions can lessen the actual larvae numbers. Be observant and watch for the presence of larvae and symptoms of feeding. Contact sprays labeled for armyworms or lawn caterpillars are best applied when large numbers of insects and extensive damage are noted.

Bermudagrass Mite

Eriophyes cynodoniensis

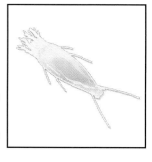

Grass at Risk: Bermudagrass.

Feeding Time: Any time during the growing season.

Overwinters As: All stages are present year-round as adults and eggs in thatch and beneath leaf sheaths.

Detrimental Stage: All stages that suck plant juices from stems and within the leaf sheaths.

Life Cycle: The adults lay eggs that hatch into nymphs in about five to seven days, and then grow into adults. From egg to adult may take only seven days. It doesn't take long for high populations to build and damage turf.

Description: Microscopic in size, creamy white, worm-like mites with two pairs of legs near the head. Not the same as spider mites. Eggs are oval and transparent to opaque. The nymphs are two-thirds the size of the adults, which are about $1/125$ inch long and whitish in color.

Damage Symptoms and Signs: Individual plants become stunted and tufted. The stems or internodes become shortened. Highly infested grass can thin, turn brown, and die. Symptoms are typically present during the warmer months. Infestations are often found near property lines and fences where mite populations build up in the unclipped grass.

Scout and Count: They are difficult to count and thresholds are normally not given. A diagnosis is usually made by the symptoms of turf decline and sections of tufted grass. Where needed, the mites can be detected with the aid of a microscope looking under a leaf sheath for the tiny mites at their various stages. Samples can also be sent to the University of Florida for identification.

Management: Keeping the lawn maintained at the recommended mowing height and mowing frequently helps prevent damaging populations. Also collect and dispose of all clippings when infestation is suspected. Apply a miticide when damage is confirmed, following label recommendations; repeat applications may be needed. Adding a wetting agent to the spray can improve control. Follow proper watering and fertilizing recommendations to help the grass out-grow mite damage. Bermudagrass varieties resistant to mites include 'FloraTex', 'Midiron', and 'Tifdwarf'.

Chinch Bug

(Southern Chinch Bug)
Blissus insularis

Grass at Risk: Primarily St. Augustinegrass, but can feed on other grasses.

Feeding Time: Hot dry weather preferred, but year-round in much of Florida.

Overwinters As: All stages throughout most of the state; adults may hibernate during the cooler winter months in northern Florida.

Detrimental Stage: All stages can damage turf by sucking juices from leaves and runners.

Life Cycle: Overwintering adults lay eggs that can hatch within a week or two during the warmer weather. The nymphs, which are red and the size of a pin-point when feeding begins, can grow to black adults with white-crossed wings in four to five weeks. In South Florida there are seven or more generations a year and in Central and North Florida three to four generations.

Description: Adults are black and about one-fifth of an inch long with white wings. The pale yellow eggs, which are laid in leaf sheaths and around nodes, are very small and seldom noticed. Young nymphs are red but so small they are difficult to see. They pass through several stages with dark bodies before developing into black adults with white-crossed wings.

Damage Symptoms and Signs: The feeding occurs primarily on the tender basal leaves. Affected grass turns yellow and then a brown straw color, forming circular to irregularly shaped patterns. Chinch bugs are best spotted at the leading edge of a bad spot in the lawn, where damaged grass meets good grass. The warmer areas of the lawn near sidewalks and driveways are often attacked early in the season.

Scout and Count: Parting the grass at the edge of an infested area is often all that is needed to see the nymphs scurrying about near the soil line. On hot days they may even be seen climbing the leaf blades and crossing sidewalks. The insects can be flushed to the surface for identification with a soapy water drench at the edge of the damaged area. You can also sink an open-ended coffee can in the same area to float the insects to the surface after filling it with water. Some gardeners have used a portable vacuum to collect the insects for identification. Usually twenty to twenty-five chinch bugs per square foot, along with visible symptoms, means control is needed.

Management: Chinch bugs are naturally attacked by fungal diseases as well as beneficial insects and can often be kept at bay. The presence of a few adults or nymphs does not always mean a spray is needed. Healthy lawns, properly watered with deep and infrequent irrigation, are often resistant to the pest. Symptoms and insect populations in the threshold range signify a probable concern that may require some action. Sprays applied as a contact application give good control, but be sure they are labeled for chinch bugs. Watering the lawn before application is also of benefit. When renovating or putting in a new lawn, look for chinch-bug-tolerant cultivars such as 'Floratam' St. Augustinegrass. Reduce nitrogen rates and use slow-release fertilizers. Also control thatch and mow at the highest recommended setting with a sharp blade. When areas damaged by chinch bugs are treated, the affected grass often continues to decline for several weeks before starting to recover.

Cutworm

Several Species

Grass at Risk: Bermudagrass, carpetgrass, zoysiagrass, and St. Augustinegrass.

Feeding Time: Spring through fall, feeding during the evening hours.

Overwinters As: Pupae or mature inactive larvae in the soil.

Detrimental Stage: Larvae severing plant stems and roots.

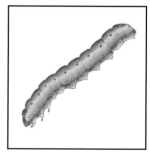

Life Cycle: In the spring the overwintering forms turn into adults to begin the next generation. The females lay numerous eggs in clusters on leaf blades, which hatch within ten days. The larvae go through several stages, feeding at night on leaf blades and returning to the soil or thatch layer during the day. They then pupate before turning into adults. As many as three to seven generations can occur per year.

Description: Adult moths are dark brown with patterned forewings and light brown hind wings. The eggs are white and round, becoming somewhat darker before hatching. The fat larvae can reach two inches in length. They can be brown, gray, or black and are usually quite dull in color depending on the species. The larvae characteristically curl into a "C" shape when disturbed. The pupa is brown.

Damage Symptoms and Signs: Stems and leaves are chewed near the soil surface. Affected feeding sites are often small and circular in shape. The areas wilt, eventually turning brown and becoming spotty in appearance.

Scout and Count: The threshold range is six or more per square foot.

Management: Control is seldom needed unless symptoms are evident, and the larvae numbers are at the threshold range. If needed, insecticidal sprays or granular treatments usually give good control. Cutworms are seldom serious pests of turf, but survive on the grass and then move on to newly planted flowers and vegetables to cause major damage.

Fire Ant

(Red Imported Fire Ant)
Solenopsis invicta

Grass at Risk: All grasses can be disturbed but injury is usually minor. Mostly they make unsightly mounds and become a nuisance stinging homeowners, visitors, and pets. They feed on insects and plant seeds, and are predators of some lawn and ornamental pests.

Feeding Time: Year-round.

Overwinters As: All stages.

Detrimental Stage: Ants defending their colonies are capable of biting and stinging several times. Some people and pets have severe allergic reactions to fire ants.

119

Life Cycle: The colony is made up of one or more fertile females, known as queens, that lay eggs; winged males; and worker ants in assorted sizes. The males die shortly after mating with the queens. The workers perform various tasks in support of the colony.

Description: A colony contains eggs, larvae, pupae, and various types of adult ants also known as castes. They look very similar to other ants, from one-eighth to one-fourth of an inch long, but live in obvious mounds when in open sunny areas. Fire ants may also live under mulches, in pots and logs, under cement, and in homes. They are very aggressive and come running to defend the colony when disturbed. Many gardeners are stung before they realize the ants are present.

Damage Symptoms and Signs: Large mounds in lawns or other open areas. Turf may be damaged by foraging and mound formation but it usually recovers. Painful bites to homeowners and pets.

Scout and Count: Any colonies noted are a problem.

Management: Gardeners need to control fire ants to protect people and pets. Home remedies and natural controls, including drenching the mounds with boiling water and using diatomaceous earth, have had varying results. Perhaps the best control is baits that the ants pick up and take back to the mounds, which destroy the queen and eventually the colony. Baits may take several weeks to kill a colony. Liquid insecticidal drenches are quicker to control individual mounds but don't always eliminate the colony. The University of Florida recommends treating the entire landscape with baits once or twice a year to eliminate as many mounds as possible. Where needed, individual mounds can

be treated if near areas frequented by pets and family members, while the baits control other colonies in the landscape. Also the university is releasing natural controls.

Ground Pearl

Margarodes spp.

Grass at Risk: Centipedegrass is most commonly damaged, but bahiagrass, bermudagrass, carpetgrass, and St. Augustinegrass have also been affected.

Feeding Time: Throughout the year.

Overwinters As: Nymphs or as cysts, also known as the "ground-pearl" stage.

Detrimental Stage: Nymphs.

Life Cycle: Adult females about one-sixteenth of an inch long emerge from the overwintering cyst stage and crawl to new sites to lay eggs. Egg laying occurs April through June. The young nymphs, about the size of sand grains, emerge during late spring and summer and move through the soil, feeding when they come into contact with roots. Once the nymphs develop a feeding relationship with the roots, they secrete a yellowish pearl-like covering over their body that grows to an eighth of an inch in diameter. Typically there is one generation a year, but they can remain in the ground-pearl stage for years depending on environmental conditions.

Description: The adult female is a pinkish scale insect with small forelegs and claws. The males resemble gnats and are seldom noticed. The egg clusters are pinkish white and enclosed in a white waxy sac. The nymphs are slender at first, later forming a hard, globular, encysted yellowish shell known as a ground pearl.

Damage Symptoms and Signs: Damage resembles drought and nematode damage, producing patches of wilting and declining turf. Affected grass is slow to recover from drought stress, and eventually yellows, turns brown, and dies.

Scout and Count: Remove a square foot of sod at the edge of an affected area and inspect for the ground-pearl stage. If present, the insects freely drop from the sod as it's being lifted from the ground. No thresholds are established for this pest, but when the decline symptoms and pearls are noted, the insects are likely the cause.

Management: No insecticide is labeled for ground pearl control. Gardeners have to rely on good management practices to keep the turf healthy and able to outgrow the pest damage. Maintain proper fertilization, watering, and mowing. Ground pearls are one reason centipedegrass is seldom planted in Central and South Florida.

Hunting Billbug

Sphenophorus venatus verstitus

Billbug Larva

Grass at Risk: Zoysiagrass, but also feeds on bermudagrass, bahiagrass, seashore paspalum, and St. Augustinegrass.

Feeding Time: Spring through fall.

Overwinters As: Adults hibernating in the grass; larvae and pupae may also overwinter.

Detrimental Stage: Adults and larvae.

Life Cycle: Adults emerge in spring, feeding on leaves and burrowing into stems where they lay eggs. Larvae hatch and feed on grass stems and roots during the growing season before they change into adults. A second generation may follow during the warmer months.

Billbug Adult

Description: Adults are black, with an obvious "Y" at the back of the head. They grow to half an inch long and are often referred to as snout beetles or weevils because of a long snout or "bill" with chewing mouth parts. Adults lay creamy white eggs in the lower portions of the plants, often at leaf petioles or within the stems, which hatch in about ten days. The resulting larvae grow to three-eighths of an inch long and are white with a dark head, resembling white grubs, but lack legs. They feed on the leaves in the crown and eventually enter the roots. The larvae change to the pupa stage in the soil or roots. They are a yellowish color, similar to the adults in shape, and mature in about a week.

Damage Symptoms and Signs: Most damage occurs in the fall and winter when there are larger populations of these insects. The damage is most likely noted when grass is under heat stress and during drier weather. Serious turf decline may not be noted until spring as the grass begins new growth. Areas of the turf wilt, turn yellow, then brown, and the grass can eventually die. In these areas, the grass can be pulled out by hand and easily lifted from the soil where the chewing has occurred. A sawdust-like material known as frass may be present on the stems where the chewing has taken place.

Scout and Count: Check unusual wilting and yellow areas by cutting and lifting a twelve-inch square of sod with a few inches of attached soil from the edge of the affected site. Inspect the roots for feeding damage and look for the white larval stage. If six to ten billbugs are found in a square foot of turf, a control is needed. A soap flush can be used to check for adults.

Management: Just because adults are seen does not mean treatment is necessary. Often they do not cause obvious damage. Treatment should be considered when symptoms are seen, insects have been identified, and numbers are near the threshold amount. Then appropriately labeled insecticides can be applied as a spray or granular treatment according to directions—usually in May, June, or July—to control the larval stage. Irrigate both sprays and granules after application with half an inch of water to move the insecticide into the soil. Adults can be controlled as needed following label instructions.

Leafhopper
Several Species

Grass at Risk: Almost any lawn grass.

Feeding Time: Throughout the year during warm weather.

Overwinters As: Eggs or adults. Often active year-round except in extremely cold weather.

Detrimental Stage: Adults and nymphs.

Life Cycle: Adults begin to feed and mate in the spring, laying eggs in the leaf blades of the grass. Two weeks later, the eggs hatch into nymphs that mature and grow into adults. There can be numerous generations, depending on the species and location within the state.

Description: Adult leafhoppers, as the name implies, hop, and fly. They are typically less than a fifth of an inch long with a triangular shape and characteristic folded wings over their bodies. Color can vary depending on the species from yellow to green to gray. The white eggs are elongated in shape. The nymphs are the same shape as the adults, just paler, smaller, and wingless.

Damage Symptoms and Signs: Leafhoppers have piercing-sucking mouth parts that extract the plant's sap. Heavy infestations can cause speckled or bleached leaf blades, which can be confused with drought, disease, or other insect damage.

Scout and Count: Leafhoppers are very common and often a cause for concern in home lawns, but no thresholds have been determined.

Management: While leafhoppers are usually numerous, seldom is major turf decline attributed to their feeding in the lawn. They do suck juices from the turf, but it is typically quite resistant. They appear to be more an annoyance than serious problem. Where leafhopper damage is determined to be causing turf decline, insecticides can be applied to reduce the populations, following label instructions.

Mole Cricket

Scapteriscus spp.

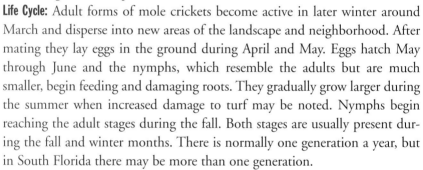

Grass at Risk: Bahiagrass, bermudagrass and zoysia-grass are likely to be affected, but all turf types may experience damage.

Feeding Time: Year-round except during very cold weather.

Overwinters As: Nymphs and adults.

Detrimental Stage: Adults and nymphs tunnel through the soil and may feed on the underground turf portions.

Life Cycle: Adult forms of mole crickets become active in later winter around March and disperse into new areas of the landscape and neighborhood. After mating they lay eggs in the ground during April and May. Eggs hatch May through June and the nymphs, which resemble the adults but are much smaller, begin feeding and damaging roots. They gradually grow larger during the summer when increased damage to turf may be noted. Nymphs begin reaching the adult stages during the fall. Both stages are usually present during the fall and winter months. There is normally one generation a year, but in South Florida there may be more than one generation.

Description: Several species are most damaging in Florida, including the southern and tawny species. The adults resemble a cross between a cricket and a mole, maturing to about one and a half inches long. They are brown with a tapered head and are well equipped for living in the soil, with mole-like front legs for digging. Gray to brownish oval eggs are deposited in chambers underground, where they hatch in about twenty days during warmer weather. The nymphs look just like the adults but are wingless and smaller.

Damage Symptoms and Signs: Mole crickets feed on other insects, organic matter, and often grass parts. The tunneling also causes considerable damage: It cuts roots, loosens the turf, and leaves the roots exposed, which causes them to dry out.

Scout and Count: Mole cricket damage is most noticeable starting in midsummer when the insects grow large and the tunnels become obvious. The damage continues during the warmer fall through early spring days. Gardeners can feel the softened turf produced by the tunneling as they walk across the lawn. Often the tunnels can be spotted on bare ground. If mole crickets are expected to be a problem, start in June to flush out the next generation with a soapy solution to get a count. If present, the small mole crickets come to the surface in less than three minutes. The soap flush can also be used at other times, but as the mole crickets grow bigger they tunnel deeper and the technique is less effective in bringing them to the surface. Usually a count of two or more mole crickets per square foot means a treatment is needed.

Management: Treat for mole crickets only when the insects are noted, the threshold count is reached, and injury is evident. Baits are effective during the summer when the mole crickets are young and coming to the surface to feed at night. Baits are best applied in the late afternoon or early evening after the summer rains have ended. Sprays and granular treatments can also be used and most should be watered in after application, but check the label. Natural controls such as beneficial nematodes and a parasitic fly can also help to control this pest. Many are already established in Florida and seem to be providing good control. Also check for varieties that are less likely to be affected by mole crickets, like 'TifSport' bermudagrass, which has shown a non-preference to this insect.

Scale

Rhodesgrass Scale (Mealybug), *Antonina graminis*
Bermudagrass Scale, *Odonaspis ruthae*

Grass at Risk: Bermudagrass and St. Augustinegrass are most often affected, but any grass can be attacked.

Feeding Time: Any time during the growing season.

Overwinters As: Adults and nymphs both overwinter in warmer locations.

Detrimental Stage: Adults and nymphs.

Life Cycle: Adults of the rhodesgrass scale give birth to nymphs but the bermudagrass scale lays eggs. The crawlers move to new locations on the grass and begin feeding. Both become immobile and secrete a wax-like covering. The mature rhodesgrass scale is covered with a cottony mass and the bermudagrass scale a hard, clam-like, white coating. Several generations can be produced in a year.

Description: Rhodesgrass scale adults are legless, purplish-brown, and have oval bodies enclosed in a white sac that turns yellow with age. The nymphs resemble the adults, but have legs and grow to about an eighth of an inch when mature. Bermudagrass scale adults lay eggs that hatch into crawlers that eventually mature into the white clam-like adults, one-fifteenth of an inch in diameter.

Damage Symptoms and Signs: Heavy infestations are usually needed to cause significant turf decline. Affected turf becomes yellow, thins, and eventually turns brown. Bermudagrass scale may be difficult to find because of the small size. Rhodesgrass scale can be detected by the white, cottony insects on the grass, which look like fertilizer caked on the runners and stems.

Scout and Count: No threshold ranges have been determined. Part the grass blades in the declining areas to find the insects on the leaves and stolons.

Management: Scale insects are less common in Florida turf but can be observed from time to time. Stay alert for these pests and check for them when other insects and diseases have been eliminated as the cause of the problem. When damaging infestations are noted, apply an insecticide following label instructions. Catch and destroy the clippings.

Tropical Sod Webworm

Herpetogramma phaeopteralis and other species

Grass at Risk: All turfgrasses, but St. Augustinegrass and seashore paspalum are favorites.

Feeding Time: Spring through fall.

Overwinters As: Tropical sod webworms are temperature sensitive, and studies suggest they overwinter in South Florida and migrate north to other areas of the state during the warmer months.

Detrimental Stage: Larvae.

Life Cycle: Adults lay eggs among the grass blades during the late afternoon and early evening. Under ideal conditions the eggs hatch within two weeks and the larvae feed on the grass blades for about four weeks. They skeletonize the leaves at first and eventually consume entire leaf blades. They complete the feeding stage and pupate for a week before emerging as adults. The life cycle is dependent on temperature and can be completed in six weeks during the summer. Their development greatly slows during cooler weather and all damaging activity is over by late fall. There can be several generations during the growing season.

Description: Several species of sod webworms are active in Florida but the tropical sod webworm, *Herpetogramma phaeopteralis,* is most prevalent. Tropical sod webworm moths are brown and have a wingspan of up to three-fourths of an inch. The larvae grow to three-fourths of an inch long and are gray-green with dark spots when at the feeding stage. They feed at night and when detected are normally found curled into a "C" shape near the soil line. The pupae are brown and found near the soil surface.

Damage Symptoms and Signs: Larvae feed on the leaf blades at night, chewing small sections at first but feeding on entire leaves as they grow larger. The damage appears as if the grass has been closely mowed, and runners are often exposed. The larvae can be detected by parting the grass blades and looking for the small caterpillars during the daytime curled at or near the ground. Green excreta can usually be found near the caterpillars.

Scout and Count: Look for areas of closely clipped and browning grass to search for sod webworm activity. Soap flushes can be used to bring the caterpillars to the surface if they are difficult to find by parting the grass blades. Threshold levels are ten or more per square foot in the larval stage.

Management: Many gardeners use moth activity as a sign that sod webworms may be feeding in the yard. These may or may not be webworm adults and even if they are, damage does not occur unless eggs are laid and larvae survive. When feeding of larvae is noted, the damage is to the grass blades and if you don't mind the close-cut look, most lawns can recover on their own with just normal care. Where needed, sprays and granular insecticide treatments can be made to the problem area and a small zone outside the feeding site. A natural insecticide containing *Bacillus thuringiensis* offers control, as do synthetic pesticides for caterpillars. Several predators found naturally in lawns, including spiders and earwigs, may also control sod webworms.

Two-Lined Spittlebug

Prosapia bicincta

Grass at Risk: All turfgrasses, but bahiagrass, bermudagrass, centipedegrass, and St. Augustinegrass are favorites.

Feeding Time: April through October.

Overwinters As: Eggs.

Detrimental Stage: Adults and nymphs.

Life Cycle: Eggs hatch in spring and give rise to the yellow to white nymphs that surround themselves in a frothy spittle-like mass. These immature stages gradually grow into adults in about two and a half months and lay eggs within the grass, near leaf sheaths or in stems. There are two generations a year.

Description: These are piercing-sucking insects with all stages feeding on the grass, but adults appear to cause the most damage. The young nymphs are small and yellow to white. The adults are up to half an inch long, black with a leafhopper look, with two very obvious orange stripes across their wings.

Damage Symptoms and Signs: The spittlebugs suck juices from the grass blades and cause reduced growth and vigor. Research suggests the adults inject a toxic substance into the leaf blades to cause decline. Severely affected turf develops yellow tips and leaves that may wither and die.

Scout and Count: Look near the soil line among the grass blades and nearby ornamentals for the frothy masses that contain the nymphs. Adults are often noted flying above the lawn during the morning hours. They may also fly up during mowing or when you walk through the grass, landing on your skin, where they can give a sometimes painful pinch. No thresholds have been established.

Management: Spittlebugs are often more of a nuisance than a threat to the grass. It appears that more real turf damage is caused in the northern portion of the state than other areas. They are usually more of a problem in turf with a thatch buildup. Following good turf care practices may help with control. They are less of a problem when the turf is under proper irrigation. Insecticides can be applied if needed.

White Grubs

Cotinis, Cyclocephala, Phyllophaga, Tomarus, and other genera

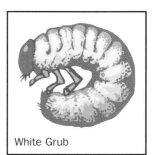

White Grub

Grass at Risk: All grasses can be affected.

Feeding Time: Year-round, but most active during the warmer months.

Overwinters As: Larvae, known as grubs.

Detrimental Stage: Grubs feeding on grass roots and rhizomes.

Life Cycle: The larva or grub stage becomes active during the spring, feeding on the roots of turf until they pupate. The adults, known as beetles, emerge during spring and summer and lay eggs to restart the life cycle. The eggs hatch into grubs that again begin feeding on grass roots. A generation may take one to four years depending on the species.

May Beetle

Description: Grubs, the larval stage of several beetles, are white with a brown head and have three pairs of legs behind the head. When disturbed they normally make a "C" shape. The pupae stage is brown and the beetles are brown, black, or greenish and may be marked with colors depending on the species. Commonly recognized adults include the May or June beetles, masked chafers, and green June beetles. Most adult beetles are about half an inch to one inch long.

Damage Symptoms and Signs: Turf affected by grubs has reduced vigor and gradually develops drought-like symptoms, including yellowing and browning of the leaf blades. Severely affected turf eventually dies as the feeding grubs destroy the turf roots. Areas affected can often be rolled back like a carpet because of the damaged roots. Adult beetles may feed on flowers and plant foliage but do not normally affect the turf. Armadillos and moles often dig in lawns with high populations looking for the grubs—one of their favorite foods.

Scout and Count: Check unusual wilting and yellow-to-brown areas by cutting and lifting a twelve-inch square of sod with a few inches of soil attached from the edge of the affected site. Inspect the roots for feeding damage and look for the white grub stage. Three to four grubs per square foot is the threshold for control.

Management: Proper care of the turf produces a root system that is more resistant to grub damage. But when thresholds are reached, an insecticide specific to the grub stage normally is needed. Timing of the control is important. Preventive insecticide treatments are best applied during late spring and early summer when the eggs are being laid. Curative treatments are applied when the grub stages are larger and feeding on the roots.

Beneficial Insects

Beneficial Insect	Feeds On
Ant Lion (Doodlebug)	Caterpillars, aphids, and many other soil insects
Assassin Bug (Wheel Bug)	Assortment of insects, but also can bite you
Big-eyed Bug	Chinch bugs, assorted insect eggs, small larvae, and soft-bodied insects
Damsel Bug	Aphids, assorted insect eggs, small larvae, and many other soft-bodied insects
Earthworm*	Doesn't feed on insects but good for the soil—too many can make the soil level lumpy, but verti-cutting the soil can help with this rare problem
Earwig	Can feed on plants, but is typically a predator and eats chinch bugs, webworms, and other soil insects
Green Lacewing	Small caterpillars, aphids, mites, thrips, mealybugs, soft-bodied insects, and insect eggs
Ground Beetle (Aphid Lion)	Feeds on almost any soil insect, particularly cutworms, armyworms, sod webworms, and small mole crickets
Ladybug Beetle (Ladybird Beetle)	Adults and larvae feed on small, soft-bodied insects such as aphids, mites, scale, and insect eggs

Beneficial Insects

Beneficial Insect	Feeds On
Minute Pirate Bug	Thrips, spider mites, and assorted insect eggs
Nematode*	Beneficial nematodes (*Steinernema* and *Heterohabditis* species) can feed on assorted caterpillar larvae or grubs, and flea larvae
Predaceous Stinkbug	Feeds on many assorted insects, including caterpillar larvae
Praying Mantis	Feeds on almost any other insect, including other beneficials
Rove Beetle	Aphids, nematodes, and most soil-inhabiting larvae
Spined Soldier Bug	Fall armyworms and other caterpillar larvae
Spider*	Feeds on an assortment of pests, including beetles, caterpillars, leafhoppers, and aphids
Syrphid Fly (Hover Fly)	Larval stage feeds on soft-bodied insects such as aphids
Parasitic Wasp	Crickets, caterpillars, and aphids

*Not technically insects, but beneficial nonetheless.

Learn to recognize beneficial insects in all their stages. A ladybug beetle larva doesn't look at all like a ladybug, for instance. Look for pictures in insect field guides or on web sites.

Turfgrass Diseases

Plant diseases are a mystery to most homeowners. They seem to show up overnight, as gardeners often lament. They are not like insect problems or weeds where you can easily see the pest. But diseases are real and they are destructive, often quickly causing yellowing and decline of the turf.

Diseases have causal agents, called pathogens, and they are often visible, though difficult to see. Plant diseases can be caused by a fungus, bacteria, virus, or mycoplasma, but with turf all you normally have to consider are the fungal problems. With organisms such as pythium, sometimes you can see white fungal portions, called a mycelium, early in the morning. You can also see the orange spores of rust on leaf blades. But other pathogens may remain hidden in the leaf blades, rhizomes, and roots.

Pathogens causing turf disease are everywhere. They are in the soil, on your shoes, and in the air. So why don't we have more disease problems? For a disease to occur, several factors must be present: the pathogen, a susceptible turf type, and the right environmental conditions. Sometimes you can plant a different turf type to avoid a disease such as gray leaf spot that, in Florida, affects some St. Augustinegrass cultivars. But at other times, a pathogen affects all turf types. Most often your best control is altering the environment. Simple changes such as reducing watering, avoiding excessive feedings, and providing more sunlight can stop a disease. At other times you may have to use a fungicide to help make conditions unfavorable for disease development.

Just as you must stay alert to weed and insect problems, you must look for the start of disease symptoms. They can often be confused with insects or cultural problems. As you walk the landscape, look for a change in the color of the turf. Sometimes just a leaf blade or two may be affected at first. Also look for rounded spots. Many diseases, such as dollar spot and fairy ring, start in circular patterns. Unlike insects, disease problems can start almost overnight. So if a symptom suddenly appears, it could suggest a disease. They are often reacting to an environmental change such as excessive rains or a change in temperature and humidity.

Sometimes gardeners can anticipate diseases. Brown patch is a fall and early spring disease, for instance, and gray leaf spot occurs only during the summer. You can stay alert to the problems and, when needed, apply a timely control. Some diseases can also be ignored. Most lawns get leaf spots, but even though they make the turf look a little unsightly, they usually do not cause serious decline. Also slime mold is a fungus you can see, but it can just be swept away and causes no harm. Become familiar with the disease profiles on the following pages to know which ones you really have to control.

Proper Identification

Identifying a disease can be difficult. They often look like other problems, including drought, insects, dog damage, and seasonal problems. You can find help in the "Diagnosing Pest Problems" and "Troubleshooting Symptoms" sections at the beginning of this chapter. Use the pictures of the diseases and related problems to assist in identification. Use the weather as a guide to diseases, too. Remember that many diseases are related to the time of the year and the stress of too little or too much rain.

If you are still unable to make a good determination as to the problem and it's getting worse, seek additional help. Professionals working at garden centers often are experienced with the diseases. If you have the problem, many other gardeners probably do, and the garden centers can suggest a control. You can also seek help from your local University of Florida Extension office. The agents are familiar with the diseases and can help with diagnosis and recommended controls. Sometimes just a phone call to the office can help with a common disease. Otherwise you may need to take a sample to a plant clinic, which is held weekly at most offices. The sample should be from the edge of the bad spot, with good turf included. Don't just take leaf blades or dead grass. The agents need a square foot of turf with about two inches of soil. They often need to see the roots of the turf to make a good diagnosis. If this is a new or unfamiliar problem, the agent may have you send the sample to the university lab for further diagnosis. The office will have forms and instructions for processing these samples.

Fungicides

We are all looking for an easy cure for diseases. Regrettably this is rarely the case with pathogens attacking plants. These organisms are usually present all the time and other factors encourage their activity. Before you reach for a fungicide, see if you can correct the environmental conditions that encourage the disease. Fungicides are available to help prevent and sometimes cure a disease, but they are short lived. If the conditions that favor a disease are always there or seasonally present, then the problem is going to continue or return.

When fungicides can help, look for the product specific to your turf problem. The specific product you need may not be available at neighborhood garden centers. You may need to look at professional grower or landscape maintenance supply stores. Often the fungicides that really work are more expensive than the common products. With all fungicides, read the label carefully to make sure you are applying the product properly and safely.

Alternative Disease-Control Products

Everybody seems to have a pest control remedy today. Some homemade remedies may be effective, but most give little or no control. By the time you apply the concoction, the disease may stop on its own as the environmental conditions change. Use the homemade remedies at your own risk. Some may burn the plants and others could be toxic to you, your family, or your pets. The safest products, some with lower toxicity, are the ones recommended by the University of Florida Extension Service and purchased at a garden center or similar supply store, with a label you can follow. Natural products include copper fungicides, soaps, Neem, baking soda, and those containing sulfur. All are toxic in some form or quantity—just read the label. Other new and naturally derived products are becoming available as older fungicides are removed from the market. Remember, to be effective all fungicides must be used according to the label.

Common Lawn Diseases

Brown Patch
Rhizoctonia solani

Grass at Risk: All common grasses.
Season of Occurrence: Fall through spring.
Environmental Conditions Needed: Humid, damp weather with warm temperatures. Turf that is overfed with quickly available

nitrogen sources is more susceptible. Lawns with a heavy thatch layer and poor air movement are also more likely to be attacked.

Spread By: Lawn clippings, moisture, and wind.

Symptoms and Signs: Some say they can smell the beginnings of brown patch infection because of rotting leaf blades. The blades become water-soaked from the activity of the pathogen and are easily pulled from the lawn. The runners are normally not affected. Symptoms appear in a somewhat circular pattern in a day or two. At first the outer edge of the infection looks maroon and then turns to yellow and brown. Often there is some good grass left in the center to produce what is called the "doughnut" effect. This disease may occur in the same spot year after year.

Can Resemble: Winter damage, nematodes, dog urine, and insect damage.

Management: Note areas previously affected by the disease and be ready with a control if needed. Brown patch looks bad but damaged lawns can recover, because the disease affects mainly the foliage. Grass often grows back if given good care. Fungicides are available to prevent the spread to nearby turf. Treat just the affected area and the surrounding grass—not the entire lawn. Help prevent infections by pruning nearby trees and shrubs if needed to encourage good air movement. Keep fall feedings to a minimum and control thatch in problem lawns. Water turf only as needed.

Dollar Spot

Lanzia and *Moellerodiscus* species (formerly *Sclerotinia homeocarpa*)

Grass at Risk: All turfgrasses.

Season of Occurrence: Spring and fall are more likely, but may occur at other times of the year.

Environmental Conditions Needed: The disease is most active during warm temperatures in the 60 to 80 degree range, when lawns are moistened by overnight dews, irrigation, and high humidity. Dollar spot is often associated with maintenance problems, especially inadequate fertilization. Lawns having nematode problems or other stress factors are also susceptible.

Spread By: Foot traffic, mower tires, splashing water, or wind.

Symptoms and Signs: Dollar spot takes its name from round dry spots that appear in the lawn, resembling old-time silver dollars. The spots are one to two inches in diameter in the finer grasses but may be the size of a softball in the coarse-bladed types. As the disease progresses the spots coalesce to form big brown areas. The spots are produced by a decline of the leaf blades. Leaf spots form on the blades, often along the sides, and eventually encompass entire portions of the grass. They often start at one side of the leaf and "pinch off" the tips.

Can Resemble: Dog urine, nematodes, gray leaf spot, drought, or chemical damage.

Management: One of the quickest ways to cure dollar spot is a nitrogen application to help the grass outgrow the disease. Thereafter maintain the recommended fertility and water program for best growth. Also control thatch in problem turfs. Where needed, fungicides can also provide control.

Fairy Ring

Chlorophyllum, Marasmius, and other fungal genera

Grass at Risk: All Florida grasses.

Season of Occurrence: Spring through fall.

Environmental Conditions Needed: Occurs in areas with high levels of organic matter. Often present where the roots of trees were left after clearing land for a home yard or recreational area. Growth of the fairy rings and mushrooms usually follows periods of moisture. A dead spot may form during the drier weather.

Spread By: Spores moved by wind and water.

Symptoms and Signs: Gardeners often notice fairy rings by the intense greening of circular areas or portions of circles in the lawn. They are often but not always accompanied by large mushrooms produced by a fungus living on decaying organic matter in the soil. During dry times the fungus may be toxic to the grass, and circular yellow or dead areas appear in the lawns. Mushrooms may also appear without any greening of the lawn. Fairy ring may occur from time to time in the same spot until the organic matter is exhausted.

Can Resemble: Spotty fertilization.

Management: Most controls involve matching the rest of the lawn to the intensely green area. Sometimes applying fertilizer helps green the rest of the lawn. Soil aeration and water can help reduce decline of affected turf during the dry times. Remove the mushrooms as many are toxic to animals. Fungicides are available but relatively expensive and only give short-term control. Some gardeners replace the soil in problem areas.

Gray Leaf Spot

Pyricularia grisea

Grass at Risk: Most grasses can be affected, but mainly St. Augustinegrass.

Season of Occurrence: Late spring through early fall.

Environmental Conditions Needed: Mainly a summertime disease during periods of heavy rainfall or over-watering. Newly sodded or plugged lawns are more likely affected due to frequent watering. Almost all St. Augustinegrass lawns have some gray leaf spot during the rainy season. It's more prevalent where lawns are slow to dry and when over-fertilized with a high nitrogen product.

Spread By: Wind, water, and mowers.

Symptoms and Signs: Leaves are mainly affected but other portions of the turf can be infected and develop lesions. Typical leaf spots are gray-green to brown and appear water-soaked. The spots are larger than most fungal diseases of this type, to more than a fourth of an inch in diameter. Gray fungal spores and mycelium may be noted with the lesions during periods of high moisture. Severely affected leaf blades yellow and turn brown, giving a scorched appearance. Plugs and sections of turf may decline because of the disease.

Can Resemble: Drought, dog urine, herbicide damage, and fertilizer burn.

Management: Reduce watering to only what is needed to maintain the turf. Avoid high nitrogen fertilizers during periods of likely infestation. May be associated with atrazine herbicide use in St. Augustinegrass lawns. Where possible select a variety of grass that appears more resistant, such as 'Floratam' St. Augustinegrass. Fungicides may be applied where needed for control.

Helminthosporium Leaf Spot

Formerly *Helminthosporium* spp. now thought to be a combination of *Bipolaris, Curvularia, Drechslera,* and *Exserohilum* species

Grass at Risk: Bermudagrass, ryegrass, and seashore paspalum are most susceptible, but all grasses could be affected.

Season of Occurrence: Fall through spring, and into summer with some grass species.

Environmental Conditions Needed: The fungal organisms are most active when temperatures are in the 70 to 95 degree range. Extremes in moisture may encourage the fungus but wet weather seems to favor infection. Stressed lawns are likely to be attacked.

Spread By: Wind, water, mowers, and shoes.

Symptoms and Signs: Leaf spot symptoms vary with the fungus species, from round to linear and purple to brown. Leaf spotting may be all that is visible. When severe, spots and patches in the lawn can develop, turning a reddish brown to straw color and producing a melting-out appearance.

Can Resemble: Dull mower blade damage or drought stress, except for the characteristic leaf spots.

Management: Remove the stress from the lawn by following a recommended fertility program, proper watering, and wise mowing practices. Some leaf damage can be tolerated, and raising the mower blade plus applying light nitrogen feedings can help disguise the disease. Increased potassium levels in affected areas can also help boost resistance. Where needed fungicides can be applied. Remove affected clippings from the lawn during periods of infection.

Moss/Algae

Several Species

Grass at Risk: Any growing in problem sites.

Season of Occurrence: Year-round, but the damp warmer months produce the most growth.

Environmental Conditions Needed: Growth is most prevalent during the rainy season when there is plenty of moisture. Excessive irrigation, heavy dews, and other sources of moisture can also encourage growth. Moss and algae are mostly a problem in areas with compacted soil and poor air movement.

Spread By: Moisture and wind.

Symptoms and Signs: Mosses are small plants with fine carpet-like stems. Some gardeners try to get mosses to grow in suitable sites where grass won't thrive. Algae are thread-like green plants that form a thin, dense scum over the soil surface. Once dried, the algae become black and crusty. Both moss and algae are non-parasitic to lawn grasses.

Can Resemble: Both have distinct characteristics.

Management: Moss is less common in home lawns but can compete with turf when present. Algae are more common and may form a slippery layer on the surface of the soil. The best control is to improve growing conditions. Prune plants to provide more light for turf growth, aerate compacted soils, and improve drainage. Some fungicides can provide temporary relief, but unless cultural problems are corrected, the algae or moss returns. Consider the use of another type of ground cover or mulch in persistent problem areas.

Pythium Blight

(Grease Spot, Cottony Blight)
Pythium aphanidermatum

Grass at Risk: Usually ryegrass used for overseeding, but all seeded grasses could be affected.

Season of Occurrence: Fall and early winter.

Environmental Conditions Needed: Damp humid conditions often provided by dew, rains, or irrigation. The disease also needs warmer late fall to early winter weather to cause major damage of newly seeded turf. Young seedlings are most at risk.

Spread By: Grass clippings moved from one lawn site to another, shoes, soil, mowers, and runoff water. The spores are naturally present in the soil.

Symptoms and Signs: Areas in the turf one to four inches in diameter or in streaks are usually affected and turn a dark green. The leaf blades of the turf become water-soaked, with a greasy look, and tend to mat together. Affected grass often falls over, creating a swirled pattern. The grass eventually yellows and turns a straw color. During high humidity, white fungal mycelium, often described as cottony in appearance, may be noted on the leaves of the affected turf.

Can Resemble: Dollar spot, dog damage, and chemical injury.

Management: Delay overseeding until the cooler late fall or winter weather. Follow recommended watering and feeding programs for overseeded turf. Fungicides are available and may help get the turf through periods of unfavorable weather.

Pythium Root Rot
Pythium spp.

Grass at Risk: All Florida grasses.
Season of Occurrence: Year-round.
Environmental Conditions Needed:
Wet growing conditions as produced by frequent rains and excessive irrigation. Newly installed sod is especially at risk because of frequent waterings.
Sod installed during the summer and kept wet by seasonal rains is more likely to be affected. Also sod installed in shady locations or areas of poor drainage and air movement is often damaged by pythium root rot. Grass installed during the drier fall through spring months is less likely to be affected.

Spread By: Movement of surface water and maintenance equipment.

Symptoms and Signs: Grass begins to thin and decline in irregular patterns, developing yellow and eventually brown leaf blades. Examination of the root system reveals brown roots that easily pull apart, leaving a hard central strand of root tissue in place. There are few if any small roots.

Can Resemble: Drought, brown patch, nematode, and chinch bug damage.

Management: Poor growing conditions are often associated with pythium root rot. Follow recommended irrigation and feeding programs. Consider other ground covers for areas with low light and poor drainage, which favor the disease. Water in shady locations only as needed. Consider delaying sodding of potential problem sites during the hot rainy season. Select grass varieties that are more resistant to root rot problems. Fungicides specific to pythium control may help get grass through periods of unfavorable environmental conditions.

Rust

Puccinia spp.

Grass at Risk: Ryegrass, St. Augustinegrass, and zoysiagrass.

Season of Occurrence: Fall through spring.

Environmental Conditions Needed: Grass growing in shady locations and under poor maintenance programs is more likely to be affected. The disease is most prevalent during periods of warm, humid weather.

Spread By: Spores moved by wind and splashing water.

Symptoms and Signs: A yellowing of the turf in patches may be the first symptom noted. Upon close examination yellow to orange-red flecks are noted on the leaf blades. Running a finger over the leaf blades brushes off the orange-red rust spores that spread the disease. Severely affected blades turn completely yellow and then brown.

Can Resemble: Pythium root rot, take-all root rot, and chemical damage.

Management: Some rust is common in lawns and can be tolerated. Usually improving feeding and irrigation practices increases vigor and helps the grass outgrow the disease. Where needed fungicides can be used during unfavorable growing conditions. Mow frequently during periods of infection and dispose of the clippings.

Slime Mold
Physarum and *Fuligo* species

Grass at Risk: All Florida grasses.
Season of Occurrence: Spring through fall.
Environmental Conditions Needed: Periods of warm damp weather. May also occur as a result of frequent irrigation.
Spread By: Wind and splashing water.

Symptoms and Signs: Slime mold appears almost overnight and is quite scary until you realize this is a harmless fungus. Slime mold lives in the soil and can enter a reproductive phase that creeps onto the grass blades. The grass quickly becomes covered with the white to gray, sooty reproductive structures. Orange, pink, or purple forms can also be found. The fungus causes no harm to the turf unless leaf blades are coated for an extended period of time.

Can Resemble: Rust, but this problem is distinct.

Management: Your neighbors may think you are nuts, but just sweep the spores off with a broom. Slime mold can also be washed or mowed off the grass blades. The fungal activity stops during drier weather. Fungicides are not needed.

Take-All Root Rot
(Bermudagrass Decline)
Gaeumannomyces graminis var. *graminis*

Grass at Risk: Bermudagrass and St. Augustinegrass, but other grasses may be affected.
Season of Occurrence: Summer and fall.
Environmental Conditions Needed: The causal fungus is a common soil inhabitant and affects grass during periods of stress often associated with warm to hot weather and periods of high moisture. Grasses suffering from poor management and pests are often affected.

Spread By: Soil and water movement.

Symptoms and Signs: Affected grass develops a less vigorous appearance, usually yellowing and thinning in irregular patches over a period of weeks. Severely affected turf turns brown and dies. The root system lacks small feeder roots, turns brown, and dies.

Can Resemble: Pythium root rot, brown patch, chinch bugs, and nematode damage.

Management: Take-all root rot is often associated with other turf problems, including root rot organisms and nematodes. All may be present in the affected turf, causing the damage. Control of all problems may be needed to prevent decline. Check growing conditions and follow recommended care to keep turf as vigorous as possible entering the summer season. Make sure mowing is at the proper height and the soil acidity is within the desired range. When decline is noted, use of liquid fertilizers as a foliar feeding can help reduce the yellowing and may extend the life of the turf until the disease subsides. Fungicides may be used as a preventative but must be applied to sites of expected decline before the development of symptoms.

Other Problems

Armadillo
Dasypus novemcinctus

Grass at Risk: Armadillos dig in all grasses looking for insects and earthworms.

Feeding Time: Early morning and late afternoon to evening hours.

Overwinters As: Present year-round.

Detrimental Stage: Young and adults.

Life Cycle: Armadillos produce one generation a year, mating in July. Four babies of the same gender are born in late winter the following year and resemble the adults. Their outer covering is soft at first but hardens with age.

Description: Armadillos resemble a moving tank as they crawl across a lawn looking and digging for food. They have poor eyesight and limited hearing, mainly relying on their sense of smell to locate their next meal. They are well protected by a tough shell and scale-like armor, with only their belly and ears exposed. The animals have a pointed head and a long tail. Armadillos usually live in wooded areas near home sites but can also be found under buildings and in woodpiles. They live in burrows when not roaming the landscape. The animals give the appearance of being slow, but can move rapidly and are adapted to water.

Damage Symptoms and Signs: Armadillos are mainly a nuisance because they dig holes in the lawn as they search for food. Their activity does ruin the appearance of a nice green lawn. Some residents also find them living under their homes, especially a home elevated off the ground with crawl spaces underneath. When armadillos have been active, their round, pointed holes become obvious in lawns and other landscape plantings.

Scout and Count: One or more may be too many for most homeowners.

Management: When possible it's best to tolerate the occasional visit of an armadillo searching for food, as elimination may not be easy. Fences can be used to keep them out of the yard and barriers can be constructed at the base of a home. Make sure the armadillo is not under the home before creating the barrier. Insecticides have been used to reduce the food supply but animal specialists often say it makes the armadillos dig more, trying to find the insects that become scarce because of the treatments. Armadillos can also be trapped and homeowners often use the services of private animal control companies.

Centipedegrass Decline

No individual pathogen has been identified and may be a combination of factors.

Grass at Risk: Centipedegrass.
Season of Occurrence: Spring through summer.
Environmental Conditions Needed: Stress conditions such as soil compaction and poor management, especially improper mowing, over-watering, or over-fertilizing with high nitrogen products. Soil pH greater than 6.5. Also the activity of nematodes and soilborne diseases that weaken the turf.

Spread By: Not known.

Symptoms and Signs: Centipedegrass that has been established for several years develops declining areas, often during the spring as new growth begins. Areas small or several feet in diameter develop a yellowing of the leaf blades. In severe cases the grass goes from yellow to brown and dies. Often the stolons are not attached to the soil and the roots make little growth, especially in lawns with uneven surfaces.

Can Resemble: Drought stress, nematodes, and other diseases.

Management: Follow good management programs with proper mowing and feeding of centipedegrass lawns. Avoid excessive applications of nitrogen and phosphorus. Also check the soil acidity and adjust the pH if needed. Correct yellowing with an iron-only application as needed.

Dog Damage

The family or neighborhood pet.

Grass at Risk: All Florida grasses.

Season of Occurrence: Year-round or when dogs are visiting.

Environmental Conditions Needed: Any time a dog walks on the lawn. Female dogs are always suspect.

Spread By: Any dog.

Symptoms and Signs: Circular spots develop a dark green to straw-brown color. The area may have a greasy look and some smell after frequent use. Lawn may grow back or permanently decline after repeated abuse.

Can Resemble: Dollar spot and chemical burns.

Management: Not all dogs cause the same symptoms and grasses appear to vary in susceptibility to the urine. Dog owners have tried feeding their pets different diets with varying results. Perhaps the best cure is to train the dog to use another area of the yard such as a mulched section. Or you could be trained to water the urine and collect the fecal matter as it's deposited to prevent the damage to the lawn.

Grass Going to Seed

Grass at Risk: Bahiagrass, some St. Augustinegrass, seashore paspalum, bermudagrass, and others.

Season of Occurrence: Summer and fall.

Environmental Conditions Needed: Lengthening days and varying growing conditions.

Spread By: Not applicable.

Symptoms and Signs: Grass sends up seedheads that may look a bit strange among the good green leaf blades. Some are tall and a foot or more above the leaf blades, as with bahiagrass, while others produce seedheads that are close to the ground, as with St. Augustinegrass.

Can Resemble: Seed production may be a typical growth habit of the turf type. Many are known to seasonally send up seedheads that have to be tolerated. Some selections are more likely to produce the seedheads than others.

Management: Frequent mowing is the best way to eliminate the unwanted seed production. With some grasses this may mean mowing more than once a week. Residents are often tempted to use the seeds as a way of filling in the lawn, but it's not recommended because of the variability of the seed and how tall the grass must get before the seed can be harvested. If seedheads are objectionable, select a grass with a decreased tendency to produce seeds.

Iron Chlorosis

Grass at Risk: Bahiagrass and centipedegrass, but all grasses could show the yellow symptoms.

Season of Occurrence: Usually a springtime problem but could occur any time.

Environmental Conditions Needed: Often a springtime problem when the lawns are beginning new growth. Iron may not be readily available or in short supply and the grass shows the yellowing symptoms. The condition is often aggravated by an application of a lawn fertilizer without adequate iron. Often occurs in soils with a high pH. Overall yellowing of turf can also occur when soils are deficient in fertilizer. Yellowing may also be noticed in lawns with pest problems.

Spread By: Not applicable.

Symptoms and Signs: Lawns develop a pale to intense yellow color, often rapidly, especially during the spring as new growth begins. Yellowing may affect small to large areas in circular or irregular patterns. Chlorosis can be an early indication of other pest problems.

Can Resemble: Nematode and disease problems.

Management: Where possible, adjust the soil acidity for your turf type following soil test recommendations. Iron chlorosis can usually be rapidly corrected with an iron-only liquid or granular product available from a garden center. Follow recommended watering, feeding, and mowing programs to ensure the best growth of the lawn. Check for other pests that may be causing the yellowing, and control when present.

Moles

Scalopus aquaticus

Grass at Risk: All Florida lawns can be affected by the tunneling.

Season of Occurrence: Year-round.

Detrimental Stage: Adults and young.

Life Cycle: Moles produce one litter per year in March, consisting of two to five young. They live in underground tunnels and chambers six to twelve inches deep. In sandy soils they are rapid diggers, clocked at up to eighteen feet an hour.

Description: Moles are insect-eating, soft, furry animals that grow to six inches long. They have a short tail and are a shiny gray color. Moles are built for digging, with strong front feet used to open tunnels, loosen roots, and redistribute soil. Their diet includes grubs, mole crickets, ants, pupae, slugs, and more. The tunnels parallel the surface of the soil, and homeowners also might notice small piles of soil.

Damage Symptoms and Signs: Moles are not plant eaters but can damage roots as they tunnel in search of insects. The roots of grasses and other plants are cut and can dry from aeration of the soil. Newly plugged turf may be totally popped out of the ground by the tunneling and left to dry. In general, damage is minimal and moles can be helpful by feeding on lawn insects and aerating compacted soils.

Management: Moles are best tolerated. You might even try getting to know the family and giving them nicknames like "Trailblazer" or "Digger." The yard usually has more moles than most people realize and, if the turf is affected, it can be pressed down and watered to continue growth. Where needed, moles can be trapped, but trapping is not for the faint hearted. You can have a professional animal control company do the trapping if you wish. Forget the poison peanuts, as moles don't feed on plants. Most home remedies of gum, grits, and mothballs are also of limited or no value. More often the moles just give up the tunnels where these items are deposited and start new ones. One treatment worth trying is a repellent containing castor oil. Several brands are available at garden centers but must be applied fairly frequently to remain effective.

Nematodes

Nematodes are small microscopic roundworms. Various species exist, but lance and sting nematodes are two of the worst.

Grass at Risk: All Florida lawn grasses.

Season of Occurrence: Year-round, but most active spring through fall.

Environmental Conditions Needed: Warm, moist soils. Some grass types are much more susceptible than others. Bahiagrass is least likely to be affected unless planted in nematode-infested soil.

Spread By: Contaminated soil, sod, or plugs. Can also be moved by equipment, foot traffic, and runoff water. Nematodes travel on their own to affect new areas of the lawn, but only a few feet a year.

Symptoms and Signs: Areas of the lawn begin to thin and develop an off color. Growth is reduced and areas of the lawn wilt before other sections. Gradually the grass declines and may die, allowing weeds to enter the bare areas. Examination of the turf finds few hair roots and a stubbing and browning of the root system. The roots usually rot during severe infestations. Surviving grass often regrows in time as the nematode population declines. The lawn may also fill in during the cooler months when nematodes are less active. Most nematodes are harmless but some feed on plants, including turf and ornamentals. Symptoms of damage can be used as a preliminary diagnosis of nematode activity, but a soil and root sample should be sent to the University of Florida assay lab for species identification and control recommendations. Nematode sample kits are available from a local University of Florida Extension office.

Can Resemble: Brown patch, take-all root rot, chinch bug, drought, and other cultural problems.

Management: Most lawns have nematodes and some will be the type that could cause turf decline. A deep, well-rooted lawn is more likely to resist nematodes. Good lawn care is the first defense. Follow recommended watering, fertilizing, and mowing practices to keep the turf vigorous and resistant to this pest. Improving soil with organic matter before installing a lawn can help but is not very practical, and is short lived in Florida sands. Chemical controls are no longer available for home lawns but researchers are constantly looking for new products, so check with your local University of Florida Extension agent if nematodes are a problem. Areas that are declining because of nematodes can be replaced by removing the old sod, weeds, and a few inches of soil. The area should be tilled and then new sod planted. Some gardeners topdress affected lawns with sand or topsoil to give the grass a new rooting zone, but the effects only last until the nematodes enter the new soil layer. Changing grass species is also a possible control, with bahiagrass the most resistant if used on a relatively nematode-free soil.

Shade

Grass at Risk: Any Florida lawn grass.

Season of Occurrence: Year-round, but most often a problem spring through fall.

Environmental Conditions Needed: Shade from trees, tall shrubs, or buildings.

Spread By: Not applicable.

Symptoms and Signs: Grass thins, may yellow and turn brown. Diseases are often associated with the weakened turf and hasten the decline. Tree, palm, and shrub roots are often visible, competing for water, nutrients, and growing room.

Can Resemble: Nematodes and most pest problems.

Management: Sometimes the best answer is to not grow grass in shady locations. In general, an area that receives more than 25 percent shade is not a good spot for grass. If you believe grass is possible, one of the shade-tolerant St. Augustinegrasses is best. Areas where shade is a constant problem are best mulched or planted with an ornamental ground cover. When you do have shade, keep the mower blade at the highest practical height, water only as needed, and follow a good feeding program. Once grass declines in shady sites, new turf may not become established even though grass is growing under similar conditions in the neighborhood. If you want to give grass a try, use plugs to see if the area can support new turf. If new sod is added, expect thinning until the grass reaches a level where the remaining leaf blades can be maintained at lower light levels.

Table 3.1a Fertilizer Maintenance Program–Central Florida[*]

Turfgrass	Maintenance Level[**]	Total lbs. of actual nitrogen per 1000 sq. ft. per year	Feb.	Mar.	Apr.	May	Jun.	Jul.	Aug.	Sep.	Oct.	Nov.	Dec.
Bahiagrass	Low	2.5		1LF		0.5WS				1LF	1LF		
	Medium	3.0		1LF	0.5WS	0.5WS	0.5WS	0.5WS		1LF	1LF		
	High	3.5	1LF	1LF	0.5WS	0.5WS	0.5WS	0.5WS		1LF	1LF		
Bermudagrass	Low	2.5		1LF	0.5WS	0.5WS				1LF			
	Medium	3.5	1LF	1LF	0.5WS	0.5WS	1SR			1LF		1LF	
	High	5.5	1LF 0.5WS	1LF 0.5WS	1SR	1LF	1SR			1SR		1LF	
Carpetgrass	Low	1.0		1LF									
	Medium	1.5		1LF			0.5SR						
	High	2.0		1LF						1LF			
Centipedegrass	Low	2.0		1LF						1LF			
	Medium	2.5		1LF		0.5WS				1LF		1LF	
	High	3.5		1LF 0.5WS		0.5WS				1SR		1LF	
Seashore Paspalum	Low	3.0		1LF			1SR			1LF			
	Medium	3.5		1LF		0.5WS			1SR	1LF			
	High	4.0		1LF		0.5WS			1SR		1LF		
St. Augustinegrass	Low	2.5		1LF		0.5WS				1LF		1LF	
	Medium	4.0		1LF		1SR			1SR			1LF	
	High	4.5	1LF		0.5WS	1SR			1SR	1LF		1LF	
Zoysiagrass	Low	3.0		1LF		1SR				1LF		1LF	
	Medium	4.0		1LF		1SR			1SR			1LF	
	High	5.0	1LF	1LF	0.5WS	1SR			1SR	0.5WS		1LF	

[*] The boundary between North and Central Florida follows state road 40 and the boundary between Central and South Florida state road 70 from coast to coast.
[**] A maintenance program should incorporate recommendations from soil test results.
[***] See the Recommended Fertilizer Amounts table to determine the quantity of formulated fertilizer needed.
LF = Lawn fertilizer with 50% of the nitrogen in a slow-release form; **WS** = Water soluble nitrogen only fertilizer; **SR** = Slow-release nitrogen only fertilizer
Note: Iron only applications may be applied as needed to renew green color without encouraging growth.

Adaped from University of Florida IFAS Extension turfgrass recommendations.

Table 3.1b Fertilizer Maintenance Program–North Florida*

Turfgrass	Maintenance Level**	Total lbs. of actual nitrogen per 1000 sq. ft. per year	Feb.	Mar.	Apr.	May	Jun.	Jul.	Aug.	Sep.	Oct.	Nov.	Dec.
Bahiagrass	Low	2.0		1LF						1LF			
	Medium	2.5		1LF	0.5WS					1LF			
	High	3.5	1LF		0.5WS	1SR				1LF			
Bermudagrass	Low	2.5		1LF		0.5WS				1LF			
	Medium	4.0		1LF		1SR		1SR			1LF		
	High	5.5	1LF	0.5WS	1SR	1LF		1SR			1LF		
Carpetgrass	Low	1.0		1LF									
	Medium	1.5		1LF			0.5SR						
	High	2.0		1LF					1LF				
Centipedegrass	Low	2.0		1LF						1LF			
	Medium	2.0		1LF						1LF			
	High	3.0		1LF		1SR				1LF			
Seashore Paspalum	Low	2.0			0.5LF		0.5WS		0.5WS	0.5LF			
	Medium	2.5			1LF		0.5WS		0.5WS	0.5LF			
	High	3.0			1LF	0.5WS		0.5WS		1LF			
St. Augustinegrass	Low	2.0		1LF						1LF			
	Medium	3.0		1LF		1SR				1LF			
	High	4.5	1LF		0.5WS	1SR				1LF	1LF		
Zoysiagrass	Low	2.0		1LF						1LF			
	Medium	4.0		1LF		1SR			1SR		1LF		
	High	4.5	1LF		0.5WS	1SR			1SR		1LF		

*The boundary between North and Central Florida follows state road 40 and the boundary between Central and South Florida state road 70 from coast to coast.

**A maintenance program should incorporate recommendations from soil test results.

***See the Recommended Fertilizer Amounts table to determine the quantity of formulated fertilizer needed.

LF = Lawn fertilizer with 50% of the nitrogen in a slow-release form; WS = Water soluble nitrogen only fertilizer; SR = Slow-release nitrogen only fertilizer

Note: Iron only applications may be applied as needed to renew green color without encouraging growth.

Table 3.1c Fertilizer Maintenance Program–South Florida[*]

Turfgrass	Maintenance Level[**]	Total lbs. of actual nitrogen per 1000 sq. ft. per year	Feb.	Mar.	Apr.	May	Jun.	Jul.	Aug.	Sep.	Oct.	Nov.	Dec.
Bahiagrass	Low	2.0	1LF								1LF		
	Medium	2.5	1LF		0.5WS					0.5WS	1LF		
	High	4.0	1LF		0.5WS	1SR				0.5WS		1LF	
Bermudagrass	Low	3.5	1LF		0.5WS		1SR				1LF		
	Medium	3.5	1LF		0.5WS		1LF				1LF		
	High	5.5	1LF		0.5WS	1SR	1LF			1SR		1LF	
Carpetgrass	Low	2.0	1LF						1LF				
	Medium	2.5	1LF				0.5SR		1LF				
	High	3.0	1LF				1SR		1LF				
Centipedegrass	Low	2.0		1LF							1LF		
	Medium	2.5	1LF		0.5WS						1LF		
	High	3.5	1LF		0.5WS		1SR					1LF	
Seashore Paspalum	Low	3.5		1LF		1SR			0.5WS		1LF		
	Medium	4.0	1LF		0.5WS		1SR		0.5WS		1LF		
	High	4.5	1LF		0.5WS		1SR			1SR		1LF	
St. Augustinegrass	Low	2.5		1LF		0.5WS				1SR		1LF	
	Medium	4.0	1LF		1SR				1SR			1LF	
	High	4.5	1LF		0.5WS		1SR		1SR		1SR		1LF
Zoysiagrass	Low	3.0		1LF		1SR				1LF		1LF	
	Medium	4.0	1LF		1SR		1SR		1SR		1LF		
	High	4.0	1LF		0.5WS	1SR				0.5WS		1LF	1LF

[*]The boundary between North and Central Florida follows state road 40 and the boundary between Central and South Florida state road 70 from coast to coast.
[**]A maintenance program should incorporate recommendations from soil test results.
[***]See the Recommended Fertilizer Amounts table to determine the quantity of formulated fertilizer needed.
LF = Lawn fertilizer with 50% of the nitrogen in a slow-release form; **WS** = Water soluble nitrogen only fertilizer; **SR** = Slow-release nitrogen only fertilizer
Note: Iron only applications may be applied as needed to renew green color without encouraging growth.

Adaped from University of Florida IFAS Extension turfgrass recommendations.

Table 3.2
Common Organic Lawn Fertilizers and Analysis

Material*	% Nitrogen	%Phosphorus	%Potassium	Availability
Basic Slag[1]	-	8-11	-	slow-medium
Blood Meal	15.0	1.3	0.7	slow
Bone Meal	4.0	21.0	0.02	slow
Compost (unfortified)[2]	2-3	0.5-1	1-2	slow
Cottonseed Meal	7.0	1.3	1.2	slow
Dried Blood	12-15	3.0	-	medium-fast
Fish Emulsion	5.0	-	-	medium-fast
Fish Meal	8.0	7.0	-	slow
Greensand[3]	-	1.5	5.0	slow
Guano (bat manure)	12.0	-	-	medium
Hoof Meal/Horn Dust	12.5	1.8	-	slow
Kelp (seaweed)	1.7	0.8	5.0	slow
Leaves (pulverized)	0.9	0.2	0.3	slow
Manure (cattle)	2.0	1.0	2.0	medium
Manure (horse)	0.4	0.2	0.3	medium
Manure (poultry)	3-5	2-3	1-2	medium
Manure (sheep)	0.6	0.3	0.2	medium
Milorganite[4]	6.0	2.0	-	medium
Mushroom Compost	0.5	60.0	1.0	slow
Peat/Muck	2.0	0.5	0.8	slow
Soybean Meal	6.7	1.6	2.3	slow-medium
Wood Ashes	-	1-2	3-8	fast

*Nutrient levels can vary widely depending on source and manufacturer

[1] Mineral by-product of the steel industry

[2] Unfortified means no synthetic or additional fertilizer was added during the composting process

[3] Mined under-sea deposits with many trace minerals

[4] Processed biomass microorganisms from sludge

Some organic sources attract wildlife that can dig in and damage your lawn

Table 3.3

Recommended Fertilizer Amounts

Fertilizer Analysis	Amount of fertilizer needed per 1,000 square feet to supply:	
	$1/2$ lb. actual nitrogen	1 lb. actual nitrogen
21-0-0	2.4 lbs	4.8 lbs
33-0-0	1.5	3.0
45-0-0	1.1	2.2
5-2-0	10.0	20.0
6-2-0	8.3	16.6
6-6-6	8.3	16.6
10-10-10	5.0	10.0
12-12-12	4.2	8.3
16-4-8	3.1	6.2
15-5-15	3.3	6.7
15-0-15	3.3	6.7
18-0-18	2.8	5.6
20-20-20	2.5	5.0

This list does not contain all available fertilizers. Choose the best fertilizer analysis for your lawn based on soil test results.

Where needed you can calculate the amount of any fertilizer needed to supply 1 pound of actual nitrogen by dividing 100 by the percent nitrogen in the bag. This gives the amount to apply to 1,000 square feet of lawn.

For example: If you are using a 16-4-8 fertilizer, divide 100 by 16 to give the amount of fertilizer per 1,000 square feet to supply 1 pound of actual nitrogen.

$100 \div 16 = 6.25$ pounds of fertilizer per 1,000 square feet.

Table 5.1
Florida Ground Covers

Common Name	Area of Florida	Height (Inches)	Light Needed	Flowers
African Iris	NCS	18-24	sun, light shade	white, blue, yellow; year-round
Anthurium	CS	18-24	shade	red, pink, white; year-round
Asiatic Jasmine	NCS	6-12	sun, shade	white; seldom flowers
Beach Morning Glory	CS	4-6	sun	purple; summer-fall
Beach Sunflower	NCS	12-24	sun	yellow; year-round
Bromeliads	CS	6-36	shade	variable; year-round
Bugle Weed	NC	6-10	sun, light shade	purple; summer
Cast-Iron Plant	CS	18-36	shade	purple; spring
Confederate Jasmine	NCS	10-18	sun, shade	white; spring
Coontie	NCS	12-24	sun, light shade	inconspicuous
Creeping Fig	NCS	8-12	sun, light shade	inconspicuous
Daylily	NCS	12-24	sun, light shade	numerous; spring-summer
Holly Fern	CS	12-18	shade	none
Ivy, Algerian	NCS	6-10	shade	inconspicuous
Ivy, English	NC	6-10	shade	inconspicuous
Juniper, Chinese	NC	12-24	sun	inconspicuous
Juniper, Shore	NCS	12-24	sun	inconspicuous
Lantana, Common	CS	18-24	sun	numerous; year-round
Lantana, Trailing	CS	18-24	sun	lavender; spring-fall
Leatherleaf Fern	CS	18-24	shade	none
Lily Turf	NCS	12-24	sun, light shade	purple, white; summer
Mexican Heather	CS	12-18	sun, light shade	purple, white; year-round
Mondo Grass	NCS	6-12	shade	inconspicuous
Oyster Plant	CS	18-24	sun, light shade	white; year-round
Peace Lily	CS	18-24	shade	white; year-round
Purple Heart	CS	18-24	sun, light shade	pink; year-round
Society Garlic	CS	18-24	sun, light shade	purple; spring-fall
Sword Fern	NC	12-36	shade	none
Wandering Jew	CS	6-12	shade	pink; year-round
Wedelia	CS	8-12	sun, light shade	yellow; year-round
Winter Creeper	N	18-24	sun, light shade	white; spring

N - North   C- Central   S- South

Bahiagrass Cultivars

'Argentine': considered most desirable with good green color and fewer seedheads

'Common': least desirable because of poor color and open habit

'Paraguay': narrow gray-green leaves, susceptible to dollar spot

'Paraguay 22': not readily available

'Pensacola': narrow leaf blades and lots of seedheads, used along roadsides, second most popular for lawns

'Wilmington': not readily available

Bermudagrass Cultivars

SEED AVAILABLE

(cultivars available as seed may also be sold as sod)

'Arizona Common': poor cold hardiness and density

'Blackjack'

'Celebration': dark blue-green, low growth habit and light shade tolerance

'Cheyenne': forage type as well as lawn grass

'Continental'

'Guymon': excellent cold hardiness

'Jackpot'

'Mirage': good cold hardiness

'Mowhawk': good cold hardiness

'NewMex Sahara'

'OKS 91-11'

'Paco Verde'

'Panama': medium texture, dense cover

'Princess': dense growth, fine texture

'Quickstand'

'Savannah'

'Sonesta'

'Southern Star'

'Sundance'

'Sundevil'

'Sunstar'

'Sydney': dense cover, fine texture

'Yukon': excellent cold hardiness, spring dead spot tolerance, slow to establish

VEGETATIVE ONLY

'Baby'

'Bayshore'

'Everglades'

'Floradwarf'

'FloraTex': many seedheads, low fertility and water requirements, some tolerance to dollar spot and bermuda mite

'Midfield': good cold hardiness

'Midiron': good cold hardiness (sometimes sold as 'EZ Turf')

'Midlawn': good cold hardiness

'Midway'

'Mississippi Choice'

'Mississippi Express'

'Mississippi Pride'

Bermudagrass Cultivars (continued)

'No Mow': minimal seed

'Ormond': early selection, poor cold hardiness, tolerant of leaf spot

'Santa Ana': increased smog and salt tolerance

'Shanghai'

'Sunturf'

'Texturf 10': sparse seedheads, medium texture, dark green color

'Tifeagle': more cold hardy, dense growth, putting green turf

'Tifgreen' ('Tifton 328'): widely used in South

'Tiflawn': good green color

'TifSport': many characteristics of 'Tifway'

'Tifway' ('Tifton 419'): widely used in South

'Tifway II'

'Tufcote' (also sold as 'Toughcoat')

'U-3'

'Uganda'

'Vamont': cold tolerant

Centipedegrass Cultivars

'AU Centennial Dwarf' ('AC-17'): vegetative only, semi-dwarf, and more tolerant of alkaline soils, limited availability

'Georgia Common': seed available, widely used, most common

'Oklawn': seed available, more tolerant of cold and drought, limited availability

'Tennessee Hardy': seed available, more cold tolerant, limited availability

'Tennturf': vegetative only, best cold tolerance to date, limited availability

'TifBlair': seed or vegetative, more cold tolerant, slightly faster growth rate

Seashore Paspalum Cultivars

'Adalayd': medium bladed

'Durban': fine bladed

'ET': fine bladed

'Excalibur': medium bladed

'Futurf': medium bladed

'Salam': fine bladed

'Salpas': medium bladed

'Saltene': medium bladed

'Sea Isle 1': fine bladed

St. Augustinegrass Cultivars

'Amerishade': a dwarf selection with good shade tolerance

'Bitter Blue': finer texture, more shade tolerant, but susceptible to chinch bug

Common: pasture type, very susceptible to chinch bugs and other pests, marginal cold hardiness, poor lawn selection

'Delmar': semi-dwarf selection with more cold and shade tolerance

'Floralawn': marginal cold and shade tolerance, coarse texture, some resistance to chinch bug, sod webworm, and brown patch

'Floratam': coarser, some resistance to chinch bug

'Floratam II': improved version of 'Floratam', with better cold tolerance

'Floratine': finer texture, darker green, susceptible to chinch bug

'FX 10': drought tolerant

'FX 33'

'Gulfstar'

'Jade': semi-dwarf with more cold and shade tolerance, finer texture, susceptible to chinch bug, brown patch, and webworm

'Mercedes'

'Palmetto': dark green, cold and shade tolerant

'Raleigh': good cold and shade tolerance, susceptible to chinch bug, iron deficiency common in alkaline soils

'Roselawn': pasture type, susceptible to chinch bugs and other pests, marginal cold hardiness, poor lawn selection

'Seville': marginal cold tolerance, semi-dwarf, more thatch prone, good shade tolerance

'Sunclipse'

'Texas Common'

Zoysiagrass Cultivars

Zoysia japonica

'Belaire': more shade and cold tolerant, susceptible to brown patch

'Cathay'

'Companion': brand name for improved 'Korean Common' selection, coarser texture (available by seed)

'Crowne': faster growth habit, coarser, and more cold tolerant

'El Toro': faster growth, early green-up, rust tolerant, best drought tolerance, mows well with rotary mower

'Empress': fine texture, dark green color, dense growth

'Empire': broader leaf blade, dark color, mows well with rotary mower

'Marquis'

'Meyer' ('Z-52') (also sold as 'Amazoy'): improved drought and cold tolerance

'Midwest': good cold tolerance but susceptible to brown patch

'Omni'

'Palisades': faster coverage, more cold and salt tolerant

'Sunburst'

'Sunrise': brand name of improved 'Korean Common' selection, coarser texture (available by seed)

'Zenith': coarser (available by seed)

Z. matrella

'Cashmere': finer texture, quicker growth, marginal cold tolerance

'Cavalier': more shade tolerant, faster growth, finer texture, tolerant to armyworm

Matrella: common species

'Diamond': more shade and salt tolerant, finer texture, good for golf courses, faster growing, poor cold tolerance

---

Z. sinica: not the same as seashore paspalum; closely resembles *Zoysia japonica* but with better seed propagation and easier handling.

'J-14'

Hybrid (cross between two species of zoysia)

'Emerald' (*Z. japonica* x *Z. matrella*): less cold tolerant, fine texture

Glossary for Lawn Care

Acid soil: soil with a pH less than 7.0. The lower the pH the more acidic or "sour" the soil. Soils are acid when concentrations of bases like calcium and magnesium are low in relation to hydrogen and aluminum. This can occur naturally in forested areas or as a result of leached soils or growing crops. Sulfur is typically added to the soil to make it more acidic.

Aeration: the process of punching holes in the soil to increase the amount of oxygen available to plant roots and correct compaction problems.

Alkaline soil: soil with a pH greater than 7.0. The higher the pH the more alkaline or "sweet" the soil. Sometimes referred to as "basic" soil because it has high concentrations of bases as opposed to acids. Lime is typically added to the soil to make it more alkaline.

All-purpose fertilizer: powdered, liquid, or granular fertilizer with a balanced proportion of the three key nutrients—nitrogen (N), phosphorus (P), and potassium (K). It is suitable for maintenance nutrition for most plants.

Amendments: components added to soil to improve fertility or structure.

Annual: a plant that lives its entire life in one season. It is genetically determined to germinate, grow, flower, set seed, and die the same year. Some plants that are perennial in their native habitats, but not hardy in another region, such as tropical plants, can also be used as annuals.

Beneficial insects: insects or their larvae that prey on pest organisms and their eggs, or benefit the garden in another way. They may be flying insects, such as ladybugs, parasitic wasps, praying mantids, and soldier bugs, or soil dwellers such as predatory nematodes and ants. Spiders and earthworms are considered beneficial also although they are not technically insects.

Berm: soil raised above ground level to create height in the landscape or provide better drainage for a particular planting.

Broadleaved: plants having leaves of wider breadth in relation to length and thickness, in contrast to grassy plants. Broadleaved, or broadleaf, weeds are typically dicots, whereas grasses are monocots. Dicots and monocots respond differently to chemical controls.

Bt: abbreviation of *Bacillus thuringiensis*, an organism that attacks a certain stage in the life cycle of some pests. Forms of Bt can be created to target a particular species. Used as a natural pest control.

Canopy: the overhead branching area of a tree, usually referring to its extent including foliage.

Chlorotic: yellowing of leaves either from pest or nutrient problems.

Clumping: a contained growth habit versus a spreading growth habit.

Cold hardiness: the ability of a plant to survive the winter cold in a particular area.

Compaction: when soil particles are packed so tightly together that air and water cannot easily penetrate.

Complete fertilizer: containing all three major components of fertilizers—nitrogen (N), phosphorus (P), and potassium (K), although not necessarily in equal proportions. An incomplete fertilizer does not contain all three elements.

Compost: organic matter that has undergone progressive decomposition by microbial and macrobial activity until it is reduced to a spongy, fluffy texture. Added to soil of any type, it improves the soil's ability to hold air and water and to drain well.

Cool-season grass: turfgrasses that prefer and thrive in cooler northern conditions. They can remain green during milder winters.

Coring: the act of mechanically removing small plugs of soil from the ground, allowing for better penetration of oxygen and water to alleviate soil compaction, and also providing lodging places for new grass seed. Typically done in preparation for renewing an established lawn or installing a new one. Also called core aeration.

Crown: the base of a plant at, or just beneath, the surface of the soil where the roots meet the stems.

Cultivar: a CULTIvated VARiety. It is a naturally occurring form of a plant that has been identified as special or superior and is purposely selected for propagation and production.

Deciduous plants: unlike evergreens, these trees and shrubs lose their leaves in the fall.

Desiccation: drying out of foliage tissues, usually due to drought or wind.

Dethatching: the process of raking or removing the mat of partially decomposed remnants of grass blades lodged at the soil surface, beneath the living grass layer. Can be done manually or mechanically; vertical mowing (or verticutting) is one method.

Dicot: shortening of the word "dicotyledon." Plant with two cotyledons or seed leaves emerging from its seed, such as a bean or an acorn.

Division: the practice of splitting apart plants to create several smaller-rooted segments. The practice is useful for controlling the plant's size and for creating more plants.

Dormancy or dormant period: time during which no growth occurs because of unfavorable environmental conditions. For some plants it is in winter, and for others summer. Many plants require this time as a resting period.

Drought tolerant: plants able to tolerate dry soil for varying periods of time. However, plants must first be well established before they are drought tolerant.

Established: the point at which a newly planted tree, shrub, flower, or grass begins to produce new growth, either foliage or stems. This is an indication that the roots have recovered from transplant shock and have begun to grow and spread.

Evergreen: plants that do not lose all of their foliage annually with the onset of winter. They do, however, shed older leaves at certain times of the year while retaining younger leaves, depending on the species.

Foliar: of or about foliage, usually referring to the practice of spraying foliage, as in fertilizing or treating with pesticide. Leaf tissues absorb liquid directly for fast results, and the soil is not affected.

Fungicide: a pesticide material for destroying or preventing fungus on plants.

Genus: a distinct botanical group within a family, typically containing several species. Plural form is "genera," referring to more than one genus.

G l o s s a r y

Germinate: to sprout. Germination is a fertile seed's first stage of development.

Grading: changing the slope of the land, usually to make it more level or a more gradual incline.

Hardscape: the permanent, structural, non-plant part of a landscape, such as walls, sheds, pools, patios, arbors, and walkways.

Heat tolerance: the ability of a plant to withstand the summer heat in a particular area.

Herbaceous: plants having fleshy or soft stems, with very little woody tissue, as opposed to woody plants. Herbaceous and woody plant stems differ structurally, in that herbaceous plants undergo little or no secondary growth, while woody plants do.

Herbicide: a pesticide material for killing or preventing weeds.

Humus: partially decomposed organic matter.

Hybrid: a plant that is the result of intentional or natural cross-pollination between two or more plants of the same species or genus.

Insecticide: a pesticide material for killing, preventing, or protecting plants against harmful insects.

Integrated Pest Management: a combination of pest management techniques used in order to reduce the need for pesticides. Also referred to by the acronym IPM.

Invasive: when a plant has such a vigorous growth habit that it crowds out more desirable plants.

Irrigation: manmade systems of pipes, sprinkler heads, and timers installed to provide supplementary water to landscaping.

Leaching: the removal of nutrients from the soil by excessive amounts of water.

Life cycle: stages in the life of an organism. With insects it is important to know the cycles of both beneficial and harmful ones, since different stages vary in their locations, vulnerabilities, and eating habits.

Micronutrients: elements needed in small quantities for plant growth. Sometimes a soil will be deficient in one or more of them and require a particular fertilizer formulation.

Monocot: shortening of the word "monocotyledon." Plant with one cotyledon or seed leaf emerging from its seed, such as with corn or grass.

Mowing strip: a type of barrier placed between the lawn and landscaped areas that accommodates lawnmower tires, making it easier to mow the lawn edge neatly, and preventing ruts or compaction to the edges of the beds.

Mulch: a layer of material over bare soil to protect it from erosion and compaction, and for moisture retention, temperature control, weed prevention, and aesthetics.

Mulching mower: mower that chops grass blades into very fine pieces, eliminating the need to have an attachment that bags the clippings.

Node: structure on a stem from which leaves, roots, and branches arise.

Non-selective: herbicides that have the potential to kill or control any plant to which they are applied.

Nutrients: elements available through soil, air, and water, which the plant utilizes for growth and reproduction.

Glossary

Organic material, organic matter: any material or debris that is derived from living things. It is carbon-based material capable of undergoing decomposition and decay.

Overseeding: distributing new grass seed on an established lawn to thicken the grass coverage or introduce another type of grass to extend the green season.

Partial shade: situation with filtered or dappled sunlight, or half a day of shade. In the South, part shade often refers to afternoon shade, when the sun is at its brightest and hottest.

Pathogen: the causal organism of a plant disease.

Peat moss: organic matter from peat sedges (United States) or sphagnum mosses (Canada), often used to improve soil texture. The acidity of sphagnum peat moss makes it ideal for boosting or maintaining soil acidity while also improving its drainage.

Perennial: a plant that lives over two or more seasons. Many die back with frost, but its roots survive the winter and generate new shoots in the spring.

pH: a measurement of the relative acidity (low pH) or alkalinity (high pH) of soil or water based on a scale of 1 to 14, 7 being neutral. Individual plants require soil to be within a certain range so that nutrients can dissolve in moisture and be available to them.

Plug: piece of sod used in establishing a new lawn. Plugs can also be grown or purchased in small cells or pots within a flat, sometimes referred to as trays.

Pollen: the yellow, powdery grains in a flower. A plant's male sex cells, they are transferred to the female plant parts by means of wind or animal pollinators to fertilize them and create seeds.

Preemergent: an herbicide applied to the soil surface to prevent weed seed from germinating.

Postemergent: an herbicide applied to already germinated and actively growing weeds to kill or control them.

Reel mower: type of mower generally thought of as old fashioned, but with new versions achieving renewed popularity. Blades are arranged horizontally in a cylinder, or reel, that spins, cutting the grass blades against a metal plate.

Renovation: renewing an established lawn, partially or completely.

Rhizome: a swollen energy-storing stem structure, that lies horizontally in the soil, with roots emerging from its lower surface and growth shoots from a growing point at or near its tip, as in bermudagrass.

Rotary mower: a mower with its blades arranged under the body of the mower, which cuts by the high speed of the spinning blades.

Runner: horizontal stem that grows along the soil surface and forms plantlets at each node. An example is the strawberry.

Runoff: when water moves across the landscape without being absorbed, because the slope is steep, the volume of water is greater than the absorption capacity of the soil, the soil is compacted, or the surface is of an impenetrable material. Runoff from areas that have had chemicals applied can cause problems in the areas ultimately receiving the water.

Selection: a variation within a species that occurs naturally due to the presence of a multitude of genetic possibilities. Over several generations plants with the desired characteristic are isolated and propagated. This process has been particularly important in the agronomic industry.

Selective: herbicides, and other pesticides, that target a particular type of weed or pest.

Self-seeding: the tendency of some plants to sow their seeds freely around the yard. Can create many seedlings the following season that may or may not be welcome.

Semi-evergreen: tending to be evergreen in a mild climate but deciduous in a rigorous one.

Shade tolerant: a plant's ability to maintain health and continue growth in a shaded location.

Slow-acting fertilizer: fertilizer that is insoluble in water, designated as slow release or controlled release, and releases its nutrients gradually as a function of soil temperature, moisture, and related microbial activity. Typically granular, it may be organic or synthetic.

Sod: commercially grown turfgrass sections cut from a field in rectangular panels or rolls, used to establish new lawns.

Soil conditioner: chemical or organic material which aggregates soil particles for improved structure.

Species: a group of fundamentally identical plants within a genus. Synonymous with the more botanically accurate designation "specific epithet."

Sprig: part of an underground root or stem that contains nodes, used to establish new plants.

Sterile: producing no viable seeds or spores, and in lawn grasses no flowers, which is an advantage since the flowers are typically taller than the leaf blades and are not attractive. The disadvantage is that such grasses cannot be bought as seed, only as sod or plugs.

Stolon: horizontal stem that grows along the soil surface. It can form plantlets at the tips of the stems. An example is the blackberry.

Synthetic: products made to imitate a natural material, as in synthetic fertilizer or pesticide.

Tamp: pressing down on newly installed sod so that the roots have good soil contact. This can also be achieved with "rolling," in which a heavy cylindrical drum is rolled over the sod.

Thatch: layer of undecayed grass found between the soil surface and the living grass blades.

Threshold: the level at which a pest becomes harmful to its target host plant. Lower levels of the pest might not be harmful.

Topdressing: the act of applying products such as fertilizer, lime, sand, organic matter, topsoil, etc. over the top of lawn grass.

Topsoil: the fertile layer of soil where plant roots grow. Sometimes the naturally occurring topsoil is inadequate for certain plants, or has been removed during construction, in which case it might be necessary to purchase topsoil from a local supplier.

Translocation: movement of water, minerals, and food within the plant.

Transpiration: water loss by evaporation from external leaf surfaces.

Transplanting: moving plants from one location to another.

Turf or turfgrass: grass used to make a lawn.

Turfscaping: wise use of turf in the overall landscape.

Variety: a group of plants within a species which have stable characteristics separating them from the typical form. Frequently used synonymously with cultivar and selection, even though there are differences in the definitions of the three terms.

Vegetative: non-sexual production of plant material typically achieved by divisions or cuttings and not as a result of flowering, pollination, and seed formation.

Vertical mowing or verticutting: mechanical act of cutting into a lawn vertically with sharp blades or tines to lift dead vegetation such as thatch.

Viability: refers to seed that is healthy and able to germinate.

Warm-season grass: turfgrasses that thrive and perform in warm southern conditions. They can go dormant during the coldest parts of the winter, then resume growth in the spring.

Water-logged: soil that holds too much water for most plants to thrive, associated with poor aeration, inadequate drainage, or soil compaction.

Weed: a plant growing where it is not wanted.

Weed-and-feed: a product that combines a weed control, usually preemergent, and a fertilizer. Timing of an application is critical since a preemergent weed control is also capable of preventing grass seed from germinating, and fertilizing before the grass is actively growing might actually promote the growth of existing weeds.

White grubs: fat, off-white, wormlike larvae of beetles. They reside in the soil and many types feed on plant (especially grass) roots until later in the season when they emerge as beetles.

Bibliography

Barbara, Kathryn A. and Eileen A. Buss. *Pests that Wreck Your Grass and Ruin Your Weekend*. SP 327. Gainesville, FL. UF Department of Entomology and Nematology and IFAS Communication Services, 2003.

Black, Robert J. and Kathleen C. Ruppert. *Your Florida Landscape, a Complete Guide to Planting and Maintenance.* Gainesville, FL: Institute of Food and Agricultural Sciences, University of Florida, 1995.

Dobbs, Steve. *The Perfect Georgia Lawn.* Nashville, TN: Cool Springs Press, a Division of Thomas Nelson, Inc., 2002.

Duble, Richard L. *Turfgrasses: Their Management and Use in the Southern Zone.* Second edition. College Station, TX: Texas A & M University Press, 1996.

Duncan, Ron, R and Robert N. Carrow. *Seashore Paspalum: The Environmental Turfgrass.* Chelsea, MI: Ann Arbor Press an imprint of Sleeping Bear Press, 2000.

MacCubbin, Tom. *Revised Florida Home Grown: Landscaping.* Orlando, FL: Waterview Press, an imprint of Charles B. McFadden, Inc., 1997.

MacCubbin, Tom and Georgia B. Tasker. *Florida Gardener's Guide: Revised Edition.* Franklin, TN: Cool Springs Press, 2002.

MacCubbin, Tom. *Month by Month Gardening in Florida*. Franklin, TN: Cool Springs Press, 1999.

Maxwell, Lewis S. and Betty M. Maxwell. *Florida Insects: Their Habits and Control.* Tampa, FL: Lewis S. Maxwell, 1987.

Murphy, Tim R., et al. *Weeds of Southern Turfgrasses*. Gainesville, FL: University of Florida Cooperative Extension Service, Institute of Food and Agricultural Sciences.

Myers, Melinda. *The Perfect Minnesota Lawn.* Nashville, TN: Cool Springs Press, a Division of Thomas Nelson, Inc., 2003.

Ruppert, Kathleen C and Robert J. Black. *Florida Lawn Handbook*. Gainesville, FL: Institute of Food and Agricultural Sciences, University of Florida, 1997.

Tashiro, Haruo. *Turfgrass Insects of the United States and Canada*. Ithaca, NY: Cornell University Press, 1987.

Thomas, Mike (Ed.). *Florida Green Industries Best Management Practices For Protection of Water Resources in Florida*. Tallahassee, FL: Florida Department of Environmental Protection, 2002.

University of Florida Extension Publications, on-line at http://edis.ifas.ufl.edu.

Unruh, Bryan J., et al. 2003 University of Florida's Pest Control Guide for Turfgrass Managers. Gainesville, FL: Cooperative Extension Service, IFAS, University of Florida, 2003.

Photography Credits

William Adams: 19, 50, 55, 84, 88, 108 (dayflower), 109 (bermudagrass, dandelion), 110 (dollarweed, Florida betony), 137, 142, 143, 146 (iron chlorosis)

Thomas Eltzroth: 28, 43, 46, 53, 57, 64, 67, 70 (lily turf), 92, 94, 96, 97

Joan MacCubbin: 105 (heartleaf drymary), 107 (woods weed), 109 (bull paspalum), 110 (pusley, yellow woodsorrel), 111 (green kyllinga), 140, 145, 150

Tim Murphy: 105 (Carolina geranium, Asiatic hawksbeard), 106, 107 (crowfootgrass), 108 (carpetweed), 110 (dichondra, matchweed)

Kevin Mathias: 105 (chickweed, henbit), 107 (crabgrass), 134, 138, 139, 141

Lorenzo Gunn: 3, 15, 30, 40, 54, 66, 76, 98

James Van Kley: 105 (Virginia pepperweed), 108 (chamberbitter, knotweed), 111 (globe yellow sedge), 146 (grass going to seed)

Kevin Bradley: 107 (goosegrass), 108 (spotted spurge), 111 (yellow nutsedge, purple nutsedge)

Clint Waltz: 135, 144, 148

Tom Koske: 80, 86

Jerry Pavia: 70 (purple heart, lantana)

Bruce Asakawa: 90

Tom MacCubbin: 82

Felder Rushing: 73

Neil Soderstrom: 147

Laurie Trenholm: 136

I n d e x

169

Index

removal, 61-62
  bahiagrass, 61
  bermudagrass, 61
  centipedegrass, 61
  St. Augustinegrass,
    60, 61
  zoysiagrass, 61
tilling, 22, 29
Tomarus spp., 128
too much shade, 101, 102
topdressing, 62-63
  rates, 63
topsoil, 22
torpedograss, 21
tree roots, 19, 68, 69
trees, 68
tropical sod
  webworm, 126-127
  description, 127
  grass at risk, 126
  management, 127
  symptoms, 127
turfgrass
  comparisons, 81
  diseases, 132-150
  pests, 98-150
    evaluating, 98-102
  varieties, 76-97
two-lined spittlebug,
  127-128
  description, 128
  grass at risk, 127
  management, 128
  symptoms, 128
University of Florida
  Extension, 18, 114,
  133, 134, 149
urea, 47
  formaldehyde, 47
  polymer-coated, 47
  sulfur-coated, 47

vertical mowers, 61
vinegar, 112
Virginia pepperweed, 105
virus, 132
walkways, 72-73
warm-season annual
  weeds, 106-108
water
  pollution, 40
  restrictions, 35
  saving, 39
watering, 27, 30-39
  new lawns, 27
  seed, 27
  sprigs, 27
water-insoluble nitrogen, 48
water-soluble
  nitrogen, 45, 48
wear tolerance, 81, 83, 85,
  87, 89, 91, 93, 95
wedelia, 71
weed-and-feed, 46-47, 51,
  110-112
weeds, 21, 22, 25, 28, 29,
  46, 47, **103-112**
  annual, 21
  cool-season, 105
  grassy, 105
  warm-season, 106-107
  winter, 106
broadleaf, 103
  annual, 106
  control, 103
  perennial, 109
control, 21, 69
grassy, 103
in new lawns, 28
killer, 46
perennial, 21, 108-110
  year-round, 108-110
wetting agents, 36, 72

wheel bug, 130
when to water, 35
white grubs, 102, 128-129
  description, 129
  grass at risk, 128
  management, 129
  symptoms, 129
wild bermudagrass, 80
wilting, 32, 33
winter broadleaf
  annual weeds, 106
winterizing, 48
wiregrass, 84
woods weed, 106, 107
year-round perennial
  weeds, 108-110
yellow
  nutsedge, 104, 109, 111
  sedge, 109, 111
  woodsorrel, 109, 110
zoysiagrass, 36, 38, 45, 61,
  77, 81, **94-95**
  advantages, 95
  common, 94
  cultivars, 160
  disadvantages, 95
  drought tolerance, 38
  planting methods, 95
  primary pests, 95
  seashore, 94
Zoysia japonica, 94
Zoysia matrella, 94
Zoysia sinica, 94
Zoysia species, 94
Zoysia tenuifolia, 94

Meet the Author

Through his newspaper writings, radio programs, and television appearances, Tom MacCubbin has helped thousands of gardeners in Central Florida. Some readers may be familiar with his "Plant Doctor" column and feature articles for the *Orlando Sentinel* while others may recognize him as the co-host of the WCPX television *Pamela's Garden,* or as the host of the *Better Lawns & Gardens* radio program. MacCubbin graduated from the University of Maryland with degrees in horticulture. Currently an Extension urban horticulturalist in Orange County, MacCubbin is also an author of several books. In addition to this book for Cool Springs Press, he co-authored the *Florida Gardener's Guide: Revised Edition,* with Georgia Tasker, and is the author of *Month-by-Month Gardening in Florida* and *My Florida Garden: A Gardener's Journal.* Other books to his credit are *Florida Home Grown: Landscaping,* and *Florida Home Grown: Edible Landscapes.*

He has been honored for his media contributions with numerous awards, including the Best Horticultural Writer Award by the Florida Nurseryman and Growers Association, as well as being granted the Garden Communicators Award by the American Nurseryman's Association.

Tom and his wife, Joan, live and garden near Apopka.